© 2009 by YouthLight, Inc.
Chapin, SC 29036

Cover Design and Layout by Diane Florence
Original Photography featuring Payton Florence
Project Editing by Susan Bowman

ISBN: ISBN 978-1-59850-057-8

Library of Congress Number
2008909437

10 9 8 7 6 5 4 3 2 1
Printed in the United States

☞ Dedication

I dedicate this book to the memory of my mother, Mary Hunter. She was an incredible inspiration to me all my life. A loving wife, mother, grandmother, teacher, singer, and church leader, she exemplified what one can do and be by calmly and intelligently setting goals, achieving them, and enjoying the little things in life. Thank you, Mom, for your guidance, love, energy, and commitment to others.

☞ About the Author

Betts H. Gatewood, Ed.S., LPC, NBPTS, is a retired elementary and middle school counselor, having served schools in SC for 28 years. Betts has been an adjunct professor for USC, and has led numerous workshops and training sessions for faculties, counselors, and parents. She has presented nationally at counseling conventions and co-authored and authored four books, in addition to this one. She and her husband are the proud parents of three adult children and two granddaughters, and reside in Fort Mill, SC.

👉 Introduction

This book has been developed to provide a sequential series of guidance lessons for Pre-K through 5 that can be used from year to year. The book includes a lesson for each grade on nine topics essential to a developmental, comprehensive guidance program. These lessons can be the building blocks of the yearly program, supplemented with other lessons to fit a particular classroom or small group need during the year.

Why use sign language to accompany the lessons? Children learn in so many ways, and are fascinated with non-verbal communication, as their language skills are still developing. They love codes, secret messages, etc. Teaching signs is an excellent way to cement the concepts the guidance leader is teaching. The sign provides a concrete way to remember the lesson with each other, their teachers, their counselor, and their parents as they internalize these important character traits and lessons. Non-verbal communication such as sign language communicates with the heart as well as the head, and what better communication skills can a counselor teach a child?

The sign language depicted in this book has been adapted from Costello, Elaine. *Concise American Sign Language Dictionary*. 1999. Random House, Inc. If one wishes to extend the use of this dynamic, interactive form of communication, many additional signs can be added as the children are ready for more throughout the year.

Using sign language also gives students the opportunity to appreciate, understand, and value the world of those who are hearing impaired. Implementing this book in classroom guidance settings presents two gifts to children: empathy for others and valuable signals and codes which can help them with normal developmental challenges. I hope you enjoy these lessons and signs as you continue to help your students grow and learn.

 # Overview

RATIONALE

This book of classroom guidance lessons incorporates a new feature in regular guidance lessons - one or more hand signs which coordinate with each lesson. Children love using sign language, and many times they "hear" what our hands say more readily than what our mouths are saying. This universal language also gives them a common symbol which can be used by parents and teachers to help them remember certain lessons and behaviors we are teaching. The book is also unique because it provides sequential, developmentally appropriate guidance lessons on nine topics from Pre-K to grade 5. A counselor or guidance teacher could use this book as the curriculum for a whole school year's classroom guidance visits, building on each other from month to month. Some of the lessons even allow the children to communicate in different ways from grade to grade, another unique feature. It would be very helpful in the busy life of a school counselor or social worker to be able to pick up one book which has fun, creative, developmentally appropriate lessons already planned for the year's classroom guidance visits.

HOW TO USE THIS BOOK

As you plan your year's classroom guidance visits, this book can be used as the backbone of your curriculum. It provides a monthly lesson on nine important topics for each grade Pre-K to 5. You will need to be prepared to demonstrate the sign language for each lesson. Some lessons teach more than one sign, but we recommend only using one sign per month for the younger grades. At the beginning of each lesson you can review the signs you have learned previously, and let the children tell you how they are using them among themselves. It would also be helpful to tell the children at the beginning of the first lesson about what sign language is, and how hearing impaired people use it to communicate.

If you do more than one classroom visit a month you can easily supplement these lessons, going into more detail on the topic and building on what you have already introduced with the lessons in this book. Since each school and classroom has its own needs and dynamics, these lessons can be used as the springboard for each topic or concept. As you get to know your students' and school's needs, you can plan additional lessons which target your specific setting. The lessons that allow older and younger students to interact are another unique feature of this book. You will find this is a fun and satisfying technique to bring your school together, to use the gifts and experience of the older students, and to encourage the younger ones. The book includes a Resources section at the back which has publisher information to help you find the books used in some of the lessons.

Table of Contents

RESPECT FOR SELF AND OTHERS

BULLYING

SELF-DISCIPLINE

FRIENDSHIP

ANGER MANAGEMENT

STUDY SKILLS AND SCHOOL ATTITUDE

CAREER AWARENESS

DECISION MAKING

FEELINGS

RESPECT FOR
SELF AND OTHERS

Respect is the building block of all the lessons throughout the year. Children model what they see. Because of this it is crucial for them to be treated with respect while at the same time understand that they too are expected to show respect for themselves and others. This life lesson starts early, and is taught daily as they grow and mature beyond the developmental stage of egocentric behavior and thought. This first lesson focuses on the concept of strengths and weaknesses, similarities and differences, likes and dislikes in all of us. As we play games, sing, do puppets, and discuss together we learn valuable lessons on accepting and respecting ourselves and others.

☞ Hand Signs* for this lesson:

RESPECT   Using right hand face palm to the left, crossing index and third finger, putting thumb over ring finger and pinkie. Put hand on right side of forehead, and bring it downward and forward, almost like a salute.

SELF   Make a fist with right hand, thumb sticking up. Starting with hand in front of body, bring hand toward chest.

OTHERS   Make fist with right hand, thumb sticking up. Place hand in front of chest, palm facing down, and twist hand upward to the right ending with palm facing up and extended thumb pointing to the right.

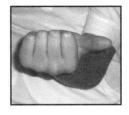

Adapted from Costello, Elaine. Concise American Sign Language Dictionary. Random House. 2000.

Lesson 1: Look What I Can Do!

☞ Overview

This lesson introduces self-respect and respect for others to very young children. Through active movement and singing the students are helped to see how respecting others and themselves can be fun and easy to do.

☞ Grade Level

Pre-K

☞ Materials

- Puppet
- *When I Was Little* by Jamie Lee Curtis

☞ Time Needed

20 minutes

☞ Objectives

- Students will learn the hand sign for respect.
- Students will recognize ways they have grown and learned since being babies.
- Students will demonstrate a self-hug and a hand shake with a friend.

☞ Procedures

- Introduce puppet friend and let puppet hug self, then hug counselor. Ask children, "What does a hug tell us?" (that we like/love each other). Let children hug themselves.
- Teach the hand sign for respect. Explain briefly that when we like ourselves we respect ourselves.
- Ask, "What do you like about yourself?" Hear a few answers then say, "Do you know how many new things you have learned since you were a baby?"
- Read *When I Was Little* or a similar book.

- Sing to tune of "Mary Had a Little Lamb:" "I can do so many things, many things, many things. I can do so many things, watch what I can do!"
- Lead children through jumping, hopping, blinking, putting on shoes, coats, etc. Let them share his/her own ideas of some of the many things they can do now that they are four years old.
- Ask children to return to their seats, and as they are settling down ask, "How do we show others we like and respect them?" Elicit ideas such as sharing, helping, and playing together.
- Encourage each child to shake the hand of a friend as they repeat after you, "I respect you and I will be your friend."

☞ Discussion Questions

- Who has showed you they like and respect you today? What did they do?
- How can we show people at home we like and respect them?
- What do your parents do that show you they like and respect you? What do your teachers do?

☞ Variations

- Let students bring in their own puppet or favorite stuffed animal, and practice showing respect to this special friend.
- Make a classroom mural of pictures of the students showing respect to themselves and/or others.
- Ask parents to send in pictures of the students as babies, and talk about how much more they can do for themselves now than when they were the age of the baby pictures. Post the pictures after children have guessed whose is whose.

Lesson 2: Our Differences and Our Sames

☞ Overview

This lesson gives students the opportunity to recognize same and different characteristics in their classmates. When children are helped to recognize and accept each other's differences, respect for these differences comes more easily.

☞ Grade Level

Kindergarten

☞ Materials

- Puppet
- Items to demonstrate concept of same and different, such as crayons, blocks, toy cars, etc.
- Colored treat such as Skittles®
- Blindfold

☞ Time Needed

20 minutes

☞ Objectives

- Students will learn the hand sign for respect.
- Students will identify same and different characteristics in each other.
- Students will develop understanding for respecting differences.

☞ Procedures

- Counselor has a conversation with puppet friend about puppet's hair being different from her friend's and she wants it to be the same.
- Look at class and say to the puppet, "Look at all the children here. Do they all have the same hair? Let's check it out."
- Ask four students to stand beside you. (These should be boys and girls with different physical characteristics) Ask class, "What is the same about these friends?" "What is different?" Help children identify these characteristics as

they study their friends. One interesting difference to show them is to ask each child to put his/her hand out in front of them, palm down. Notice the different skin tones of each; none are ever exactly the same.

- Teach the hand sign for respect to class and puppet. Tell them how important it is to like and respect ourselves and others.
- Show children plastic bags with colored treats in them. Point out the different colors. Ask children, "Do they all taste the same?" Blindfold one child and put two different colored treats in his/her mouth one at a time. Ask him/her what color he/she is eating. When he/she cannot tell you, comment that what's on the inside is what is important, not the color of the treat. Remind children that people are that way too. We need to respect everyone, whether we are the same or not.
- Review hand sign for respect and give each child a few treats as a closing activity.

☞ Discussion Questions

- What is one difference between you and the person sitting beside you? What is one thing that is the same?
- How do adults show respect to each other?
- How do you feel when someone respects you and listens to you?

☞ Variations

- Bring in pictures of people from other countries showing respect and compare the various ways different cultures show respect.
- Use the sign language for respect from time to time when you see a child showing respect to another.

Lesson 3: "I Like Myself Because I'm ME!"

☞ Overview

This lesson encourages children to learn more about themselves and their classmates. With self-knowledge and knowledge of those around you comes an increased appreciation and respect for self and others.

☞ Grade Level

1st

☞ Materials

- *I Like Myself* by Karen Beaumont
- Construction paper cut in squares large enough for child's handprint
- Markers and scissors

☞ Time Needed

30 minutes

☞ Objectives

- Students will learn the hand signs for self-respect and respect for others.
- Students will make handprints to put up around room.
- Students will discover a variety of their classmates' favorite activities.

☞ Procedures

- Teach the hand signs for self, respect, and others. Discuss the meaning of these words with them.
- Read *I Like Myself* by Karen Beaumont. Lead discussion of the theme of book that we can like and respect ourselves and others, even though we are not all alike and may look different from each other.
- Give out construction paper squares and help children trace around their hands and cut them out.

- Instruct each child to write his or her name on the thumb of the hand, then on the palm draw a picture of a favorite activity he or she likes to do. Help students get started by suggesting a few such as running, climbing trees, playing with their dog, playing soccer or another ball game, singing, reading, drawing, etc. Counselor can walk around during this activity and help and encourage children to make their own decision, not to draw what the person beside them is drawing.
- Gather children in a group on the floor and have each child share his/her handprint as you tape it on the wall, making a big circle of handprints around the classroom.
- Explain that part of showing respect for yourself and others is listening to each other and when you take your turn being proud of your work. As children share point out the variety of special activities children in this class like to do. Give a cheer as each child finishes his/her presentation.
- Review hand signs for self-respect and respect for others before you leave. Ask children to tell you some specific times during today's lesson when they saw someone showing respect for themselves or another student. You can also point out these specific instances to reinforce this behavior.

☞ Discussion Questions

- Do you and your best friend like all the same things?
- How do you feel when someone is interested in what you like to do?
- What did you learn today about a classmate that you did not already know?

☞ Variations

- Team up with another 1st grade teacher and share each classes' hand prints before you put them up in the room. Continue the discussion about the many interests and talents we all have.
- Devise a worksheet for the students as homework to have their parents complete, sharing their talents and interests. Share these with the class.
- Quietly put a token in a jar when you see a student showing respect to another, and reward the class when jar is full. It is important that you do not talk when you do this, just get the child's attention so that he/she will realize that you noticed their behavior.

Lesson 4: Collage of Respect

 Overview

This lesson helps children identify specific acts of respect. When they see concrete examples of what respect "looks like," it is easier to practice the behavior themselves.

 Grade Level

2nd

Materials

- Old magazines
- Scissors
- Glue
- Large circle of bulletin board paper
- Digital camera

Time Needed

30 minutes

 Objectives

- Students will learn the hand signs for self-respect and respect for others.
- Students will demonstrate understanding of respectful acts by identifying pictures showing respect.
- Students will create a class collage showing acts of respect.

Procedures

- After writing words "self," "respect," and "others" on the board, lead a discussion about the meanings of these words. Ask children to tell you examples of when they have respected themselves and/or others. Give examples to get them started.
- Teach students the hand signs for self-respect and respect for others.

- Divide children into small groups of 3-4 and distribute magazines to each group. Instruct students to find pictures of people showing respect to each other and themselves and cut them out. Tell them you will be watching to see how they show respect as they work together and will take pictures of examples of this.
- As you walk around and monitor, ask students how different pictures are showing respect to make sure they understand what "respect" looks like. Take a picture of each group, telling them specifically what it is they are doing that shows respect.
- Ask each group to report to class about their pictures as they glue them on the large piece of bulletin board paper, making a class collage of respectful acts.
- Print the class pictures taken, add them to collage, and hang collage in hall for others to see.
- Review the hand signs in closing.

☞ Discussion Questions

- What was the hardest part of working together in a small group for this project?
- What was the best part of this activity?
- How did students in your small group show respect for each other as you worked?

☞ Variations

- Invite a younger class to look at your collage, and ask students to explain the signs of respect they found.
- Continue taking pictures of the class showing respect when they do not expect it so that they will continue to be positively reinforced for this behavior.

Lesson 5: License to Be Me!

 ## Overview

This lesson gives the students the opportunity to make their own license which states specific information that makes them unique. In addition to celebrating their own unique qualities they are also able to appreciate specific qualities and information about their classmates, thus encouraging respect for each other.

 ## Grade Level

3rd

 ## Materials

- Blank 4" x 6" index cards (prepared as shown on next page)
- Markers
- Digital camera
- Your personal driver's license

 ## Time Needed

30 minutes

 ## Objectives

- Students will learn the hand signs for self-respect and respect for others.
- Students will make their own "License To Be ME" on an index card.
- Students will demonstrate interest in other's cards, and understand this is a way to show respect.

Procedures

- Lead a short discussion on the meanings of self-respect and respect for others. Teach the hand signs for the two concepts.
- Introduce idea that to have self-respect we need to know and appreciate who we are on the inside, what we like and dislike, what our hopes and wishes are. This makes each of us a Me.

- Show students your license to drive a car and tell them today they are going to make a "License To Be ME!" Give out index cards which you have prepared as shown on next page.
- Have students fill in name, address, birthday, strengths, interests, and one wish. Students will find it helpful for you to list some examples of strengths and interests on the board before they start.
- As they are working move around room helping those who need it, as well as taking everyone's picture to paste on the bottom right corner of license.
- Take up cards, mix them up, and read each aloud asking students to identify whose card it is by hearing the different qualities of various classmates.
- Take cards with you to put pictures on, then return them for students to keep, reinforcing concept of individual personalities but respect for all and self.
- Review the hand signs, and encourage them to use them around school with each other as they see someone showing respect for self or another person.

☞ Discussion Questions

- Do you really need a license to be yourself? Why or why not?
- What did you learn about some of your classmates that you did not already know?
- How does it feel to have classmates interested in what you wrote on your license?
- Who else would be interested in reading your license?

☞ Variations

- Divide the class into groups of three or four and let them share their cards.
- Keep the cards for a few months, and before you return them to the students to keep, discuss if everything they wrote on their card is still what they would say. Help them see how our personal interests and wishes change as we continue to grow and mature.

19

Lesson 5: License to Be Me!

✂ Activity

A finished license will look like the one below. You can either have the students print the format on the cards, or you can copy the blank format on the next page and glue on the blank index cards before giving them to the students. You could also copy the blank format on cardstock, two to a page, and cut apart.

STATE OF _____

License To Be ME

Smith, Mary _____   **DOB:** Jan. 1, 2012 _____

100 Main St _____

Timbucktu, SC _____

Strengths: good reader, good at soccer, has lots of friends _____

_____

Interests: sports, horses, music _____

_____

One Wish: I wish that I could have a horse some day. _____

(Glue Small Picture Here.)

STATE OF _____

License To Be ME

_____   DOB: _____

_____

_____

Strengths: _____

_____

Interests: _____

_____   ┌─────────────┐
                                                    │   │
One Wish: _____   │ _(Glue Small │
                                                    │ Picture Here.)_ │
_____   │   │
                                                    └─────────────┘

STATE OF _____

License To Be ME

_____   DOB: _____

_____

_____

Strengths: _____

_____

Interests: _____   ┌─────────────┐
                                                                  │   │
_____   │ _(Glue Small │
                                                                  │ Picture Here.)_ │
One Wish: _____   │   │
                                                                  └─────────────┘
_____

Lesson 6: Me, You, and an Interview

☞ Overview

This lesson gives students practice in listening to each other. As they learn new information about their classmates, they gain empathy and understanding for each other which leads to increased respect for others.

☞ Grade Level

4th

☞ Materials

- One interview sheet for each student
- Pretend microphone or one made with toilet paper tube and ball of tin foil taped on top

☞ Time Needed

30 minutes

☞ Objectives

- Students will learn the hand signs for self-respect and respect for others.
- Students will demonstrate good listening skills as they interview each other.
- Students will recognize and celebrate differences in each other.

☞ Procedures

- Lead short discussion on the meaning of self-respect and respect for others.
- Ask a few students to give specific examples of when they experienced respect from another and how it felt. Point out that one way to show respect is to listen to each other as classmates, celebrating the differences that make us special. Teach the students the hand signs for self, respect, and others.
- Ask students what an interview is. Where do they see interviews? Have they ever done an interview? Mention the word reporter as part of this discussion.
- Explain that today they will each be a reporter interviewing a classmate.

- Divide class into groups of 2 so that each student has a partner. If you have an uneven number, make one group of 3.
- Give each student a copy of the interview sheet and allow about 5 minutes per interview.
- As they are interviewing each other, walk around room and listen, helping when needed.
- After about 10 minutes give each group of 2 a turn to introduce their partner to the class, using the information gained during the interview. Each reporter can use the microphone as he or she tells class about their interviewee.
- Close the lesson with cheers for each other, and a reminder to use the new hand signs as they experience and show respect for self and others.

☞ Discussion Questions

- Did you find out anything about someone else that is the same as you?
- What happens when we get to know each other better?
- Did you learn anything new about someone you thought you knew already?
- Did you learn anything new about yourself?

☞ Variations

- Involve the classroom teacher by asking him/her to give another interview sheet to the students for homework. Ask them to interview an adult they know and trust and have the class share their interviews.
- Have the students complete the interview sheet on themselves. Keep the papers until the end of the year, then return them for the students to see what has changed in their answers.

Lesson 6: Me, You, and an Interview

Name _____

Two things you really like to do _____

_____

Favorite subject in school _____

Special person in your life _____

If you could be an animal, what would you be? Why? _____

_____

A job you would like to have some day _____

A movie you liked was _____

Your pets or a pet you would like to have _____

A favorite place to go on vacation _____

One thing you need to practice to get better at is _____

Lesson 7: Pieces of Me!

 ## Overview

During this lesson students create their own personal puzzle of themselves. This gives them a concrete way to see how multi-faceted we all are. With this understanding comes the awareness that all of us are interesting and worthy of respect.

 ## Grade Level

5th

 ## Materials

- A Puzzle
- Cardboard or construction paper for each student
- Markers and scissors

 ## Time Needed

30 minutes

 ## Objectives

- Students will learn the hand signs for self-respect and respect for others.
- Students will identify parts of themselves which make their whole person.
- Students will demonstrate respect for others by listening as they share information.

Procedures

- Lead discussion of meaning of self-respect and respect for others. Allow them to give examples when they have felt respected and when they have respected someone else. Bring in concept of differences in each other, and the need to respect our differences.
- Teach the hand signs for respect, self, and others.
- Show the puzzle you have brought and ask, "How is this puzzle like us?"
- Entertain various answers making sure they understand that the puzzle has many parts to make the whole, and without one part it is not complete.

Lesson 7: Pieces of Me! *(continued)*

- Say to students, "We also have many parts, and today we are going to focus on some of them and learn some ways we are the same and some ways we are different."
- Demonstrate on the board or overhead how they can create puzzles on their cardboard or construction paper by using pencil and drawing curvy lines on the page. Encourage them to have at least 8 parts in their puzzles. (see sample on next page.)
- On board or overhead write the following:
    Name
    A major interest
    Eye and hair color
    Place in family (only child, oldest, youngest, etc.)
    A strength
    A wish
    Something that always makes me happy
    Something that makes me mad
- Ask students to fill in the above information on their puzzle pieces. As they work, walk around room, helping as needed.
- When all students are finished, give them the option to share their puzzles and remind them that listening to and being interested in others is a way to show respect.
- Help them understand that our own puzzle will be unique, and no one else's pieces will fit in just the same way.
- Review the hand signs for self-respect and respect for others.

☞ Discussion Questions

- If someone has the same information as you on one puzzle piece, does that mean it would fit into your puzzle? Why or why not?
- Would someone's puzzle be the same if they did this activity in a year? Why or why not?
- Were any of the pieces hard for you to fill in? Which ones?

☞ Variations

- Give the students the option to draw the information in each piece instead of writing it if they wish.
- To encourage additional class bonding, group the students in small groups to discuss common interests and wishes.

✎ Lesson 7: Pieces of Me!

Puzzle

Pieces
of Me!

Dear Parents,

This year during your child's classroom guidance lessons we are going to be learning simple sign language to accompany each lesson. Each time I visit the classroom I will send home a letter telling you what we talked about and encouraging you to ask your child questions about the lesson and to show you the sign language learned that day. Why sign language? Children respond to nonverbal communication sometimes even more than our words when we need to remind them of appropriate behavior. They need constant reminders and models of respectful, courteous behavior, and hand signs are another tool we can use. They are also a lot of fun!

Today's lesson was on respect for self and others. When children understand their own strengths, abilities, and worth they can find it in others as well. Our lesson focused on how each of us is unique and has many interesting qualities. We also focused on the fact that we all have differences, and that is a good thing. When children are taught to appreciate ourselves and each other for how we act, talk, and think we can move away from some of the problems that occur when they think there is only one right way to look, think, be, and feel.

I hope you will ask your child about the guidance lesson they had today and to teach you the new hand sign. Please call me if you have any questions or concerns I can help you with.

Sincerely,

Your School Counselor

BULLYING

The lessons on bullying are an excellent follow –up to the respect lessons previously taught. The children have been using their self-respect and respect for others hand signs during the month, so they are already thinking about their behaviors and words in terms of what is respectful and what is not. The problem of bullying has reached giant proportions in the past five years, and bullies and victims alike are being emotionally and physically scarred because of this damaging behavior. We know that in every school there are three populations involved in this problem: the bullies, the victims, and the ones who just want to stay out of it and not become the next victim, the bystanders. With the older students, this is addressed so that each child can think about where he or she is in the triad and identify strategies to help themselves and others with this problem.

☞ Hand Sign* for this lesson:

BULLY   Hold both hands in front of each side of the forehead, index fingers pointing toward each other and palms facing in, thumbs are up and other three fingers are tucked into palm. Bring the hands outward away from each other a short distance, indicating a "big head."

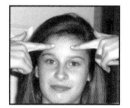

Adapted from Costello, Elaine. Concise American Sign Language Dictionary. Random House. 2000.

Lesson 8: Taking Care of Me

 Overview

This lesson helps young children understand that they do not have to allow another child to be rough with them. Through role play and puppets they see examples of appropriate and inappropriate behavior, and are encouraged to tell an adult if they need help.

Grade Level

Pre-Kindergarten

Materials

- Two puppets, one cuddly and soft like a bear or puppy and one rubbery and hard like a shark or wolf

Time Needed

20 minutes

Objectives

- Students will learn the hand sign for bully.
- Students will practice kind and unkind ways to act with each other.
- Students will learn what to do if someone is hurting them.

Procedures

- Introduce the two puppets. Ask children which puppet looks like he would be a good friend and someone they would want to play with.
- Explain that there are ways we can act like the teddy bear and there are ways we can even act like the shark.
- Ask them if they have ever heard the word "bully." Lead a short discussion listening to their understanding and then making sure they realize what a bully is.

- Explain that a bully would do things more like the shark. Act out specific examples using the puppets; i.e. the shark jerks something away from the teddy bear; the shark pushes the bear out of the way so he can go first; the shark calls the bear "dummy;" etc. Use examples the children have told you, if appropriate.
- Talk about how important it is to tell a grown-up if another child is hurting you and being a bully. Role play this with shark puppet calling teddy bear a name and let the teddy bear tell you about it.
- Let a few volunteers come to the front to role play telling you when the shark puppet is unkind to them.
- Teach children the hand sign for bully, and encourage them to use the sign or their words if someone is bullying them.

☞ Discussion Questions

- Who are some adults you could tell if someone is being mean to you?
- How do you feel when someone acts like a bully? What could you say to the bully?
- What could you do if you see a friend being bullied?

☞ Variations

- Set up a drawing center in the classroom, and ask the children to draw pictures of themselves telling a trusted adult about a bully problem.
- Give every child a teddy bear sticker to remind them to treat each other kindly.

Lesson 9: Pom Poms Rule!

 Overview

Concrete objects help younger children understand more abstract concepts. In this lesson rocks and pom poms are used to demonstrate the difference between friendly and non-friendly behaviors. Children have an opportunity to role play to further their understanding of respectful ways to treat others.

 Grade Level

Kindergarten

 Materials

- Bag of colorful pom poms (or cotton balls)
- Bag of rocks with pointed edges, not smooth (can be bought at a dollar store)

 Time Needed

20 minutes

Objectives

- Students will learn the hand sign for bully.
- Students will recognize the difference between soft and hard.
- Students will relate soft and hard to how to treat people.

Procedures

- Remind students of the hand signs from last month, self-respect and respect for others. Lead a short discussion on specific ways they are showing respect for each other.
- Introduce the word "bully" and ask children what this word means. Elicit examples of bully behavior and guide them in identifying what this is.
- Teach the hand sign for bully, and tell them this is what today's lesson is about.
- Bring out pom poms and rocks, and give each student one of each.

- Ask them how each feels, and elicit adjectives such as soft, comforting, light, and friendly for the cotton ball and hard, sharp, pointy, and uncomfortable for the rock.
- Ask them if bully behavior would be a rock or a pom pom.
- Announce that we are going to practice ways to get along with our friends and siblings and decide if each is a pom pom way or a rock way.
- Ask volunteers to help you act out the following scenarios, first in a rock/bully way then in a pom pom way.

<u>Scenarios:</u>
- You are playing with another student and you want the truck he/she is playing with.
- You are tired of waiting for the swing on the playground, and the person in it has had a long turn already.
- The teacher tells you to line up at the door and you want to be first today.
- Your mother leaves the room and your little brother grabs the book you are holding.
- The team that "always" wins finally loses to your team, and you say to them, "………………….."
- Another student is having trouble writing the letter B. You are sitting next to him/her at the writing center. What do you do or say?

- Take up the rocks, but leave the pom poms with the students to remind them to use pom pom behavior, not rock behavior.
- Review the sign language for bully and encourage them not to be rock hard bullies!

☞ Discussion Questions

- Who are some adults you trust who you can tell if you are having a problem with a bully?
- What could you do if you see another child being bullied?
- Why do you think some children act like bullies sometimes?

☞ Variations

- Ask the classroom teacher to put pom poms in a jar in the class each time she sees a student treating another in a friendly way. Reward class with extra recess when the jar is full.
- Ask the students to give some examples of bully behaviors they have experienced. Role play these with helpful ideas of what they could do in each situation.

Lesson 10: To Tell Or Not To Tell

 Overview

Children need guidance in understanding the difference between tattling and telling an adult important information. This lesson helps them understand the difference by citing twenty different situations and making a game out of determining if the child should tell or not.

Grade Level

1st

Materials

• Two signs that you have created, one will say TELL and one will say TATTLE.

Time Needed

20 minutes

Objectives

• Students will learn the hand sign for bully.
• Students will identify times they need to tell the teacher and times they need to handle the problem independently.
• Students will be able to cite specific examples of bully behavior.

Procedures

• Ask students, "What is a bully?" "Has a bully ever bothered you?" "What did he or she do or say?" (Remind students that we will not be using specific names as we describe our problems with a bully.) Tell them that the definition of bully behavior is "repeated behavior with intent to harm or injure."
• Teach students the hand sign for bully. Tell them this will be a new code we can use here at school if we need help when someone is bullying us. Remind them that it is always important to tell an adult, either with words or a sign, that we need help.

- Say to the children, "Do children sometimes tell an adult when they could handle the problem themselves? Today we are going to play a game to help us learn the difference between times we need to tell and times we do not. What do we call it when we tell on someone and they were not hurting us, but just bugging us? That's right, that is called tattling. When we tattle we just want to get someone in trouble, but when we tell on a bully we want to help someone else or ourselves not be hurt."
- Read the attached examples of behaviors first graders might encounter in the course of the school day. Each student gets a turn. If he or she thinks it is a bully behavior that they need to tell an adult they are to stand under the sign you have put on the board which says TELL! If he or she thinks it is a behavior that annoys you and you want the other student to get in trouble they are to stand under the sign that says TATTLE.
- After each child has had a turn to stand in a particular spot explain that there are more children on the side of the tattling. That is because there are more nice children than bullies at our school. We do not need to be afraid of a bully, just ready to take care of ourselves and others by telling an adult when a bully is bothering you or you see a bully bothering someone else.
- Review the hand sign for bully in closing lesson.

☞ Discussion Questions

- Name some trusted adults you could tell if you are being bullied.
- Is it sometimes hard to tell the difference between telling on a bully and tattling? Why or why not? What should we do if we are not sure?
- How do you feel when someone tattles on you?

☞ Variations

- Allow the children the opportunity to suggest some other situations that could be either tattling or telling.
- Instead of each student having a turn individually, put students in small groups of 3-4. Let students discuss each situation first before going to the appropriate sign as a small group.

Lesson 10: Telling or Tattling?

✂ Activity

Please print these situation cards out and put in random order as the game is played.

(Note to counselors: Numbers 3,7,10,13,16, and 17 are situations an adult should be made aware of.)

1. Your sister takes too long brushing her teeth and you can't get to the sink.

4. In the cafeteria at breakfast another student pushes ahead of you in line.

7. On the way to the classroom a boy grabs the apple you brought to the teacher and doesn't give it back.

2. You forget your math book, and your friend on the bus says, "Well, that was dumb. Now you'll have to miss recess."

5. You spill your milk and two girls laugh at you.

8. In the classroom you can't find your pencil and the girl across the table laughs at you.

3. A kid on the bus steps on your foot hard, on purpose. He has done this other times as well.

6. A friend tells you she isn't going to play with you today, but doesn't tell you why.

9. You have on a new shirt and a boy in the room says it is ugly.

13. You fall off the monkey bars and another kid pushes you back down when you try to stand up.

17. A student across from you in class tells you if you don't let him/her copy your spelling paper he/she will get you after school.

10. In art class another student takes the paint when the teacher isn't looking and marks all over your picture.

14. While on the swing the friend pushing you doesn't stop when you tell him/her you are ready to get off.

18. On the way to the bus to go home you drop a book and the next person in line steps on it.

11. At lunch someone calls you "slowpoke" because you can't decide what you want.

15. You get pushed in line because someone at the back of the line falls down.

19. At the bus stop in front of your house a neighbor kid calls you a "wimp."

12. On the playground another kid says you can't play soccer because you are not fast enough.

16. When you get back in the class you see another student taking your markers out of your desk and putting them in his/her desk.

20. In the kitchen at home your brother takes the biggest piece of brownie.

Lesson 11: Be Proud in a Crowd

☞ Overview

In this lesson students are introduced to a unique and likeable little girl who gives them excellent guidance in handling a bully. Using humor, but not minimizing the potential harm a bully can do, the lesson provides real and practical strategies to use when encountering a bully.

☞ Grade Level

2nd

☞ Materials

- *Stand Tall, Molly Lou Mellon* by Patty Lovell

☞ Time Needed

30 minutes

☞ Objectives

- Students will learn the hand sign for bully.
- Students will be able to cite specific examples of bully behavior.
- Students will identify four ways to stay strong when someone is trying to bully them.
- Students will practice positive strategies to use when encountering a bully.

☞ Procedures

- Discuss the meaning of the words bully, target, and victim. Remind children, "We are not going to use specific names, but if you want to tell a time when you felt like you were bullied you can tell us exactly what happened to you."
- Help them see that one can be a target, but not become a victim. After a short discussion tell children you are going to share a story with them about a little girl who was neither big nor strong, powerful nor perfect, but who handled a bully without becoming a victim. Ask them to listen carefully to how she did it.
- Read *Stand Tall, Molly Lou Mellon*. Use the following questions to help the children process the book.

- What are the four things Molly Lou's grandmother told her to do?
  As the children answer, list on the board:
  1. walk proudly
  2. smile big
  3. sing out clear and strong
  4. believe in yourself.
- How did this advice help Molly Lou? Was she a target? A victim? Why not?
- Who was the bully in the book?
- What did he do that made him a bully?
- Was he a bully at the end of the book? Why not?
- Repeat the examples of the specific times someone was bullied mentioned at the beginning of the lesson and ask the children how Molly Lou might have handled the situation.
- Lead volunteers in role plays of the different ways to handle bully behavior.
- Encourage them to help each other by using the sign language when they see bully behavior and thinking of how to be more like Molly Lou. Also remind students to go to a trusted adult if someone is hurting them and they need help. It is always OK to tell an adult, and they can help you figure out the best thing to do.
- Close the lesson with each child standing tall and walking in place at their desks smiling big, and singing out clearly and strong, "I believe in myself."

☞ Discussion Questions

- What is the difference between being a target and being a victim?
- How can you help yourself and others not be a victim of a bully?
- Name some trusted adults you can go to if you are being bullied?

☞ Variations

- Give each child a note card to write down the names of trusted adults they could report a bully to and instruct them to put this note card in a safe place in their book bags or desks. On the other side of the card have them write the four things Molly Lou's grandmother told her to do (see # 2 above).
- Lead children in Molly Lou's motto, "I believe in myself" at least once a week.

Lesson 12: Bully or Bossy?

 Overview

This lesson helps children differentiate between being bossed and being bullied, an important distinction. The lesson incorporates a fun game to help them learn the difference, as well as what to do in each situation.

Grade Level

3rd

Materials

- Index cards, one for each student
- BULLY and BOSSY signs

Time Needed

30 minutes

Objectives

- Students will learn the hand sign for bully.
- Students will identify examples of both being bullied and being bossed.
- Students will develop strategies to handle both bullies and bossy friends.

Procedures

- Teach students the hand sign for bully. Remind them of last month's signs, respect for self and others, and lead a short discussion on how respect relates to today's lesson on bullies.
- Give students an index card and ask them to write four examples of bossy behavior on one side and four examples of bully behavior on the other. Put some specific examples on the board to get them started thinking such as: wanting to be first all the time; telling you who you should play with; always wanting to be the leader in a game; pushing you down in line, etc.

- Collect the cards and divide the class into four teams of 5 or 6 students each. Designate two sides of the class with the signs - a cow labeled BOSSY and a bull labeled BULLY.
- Read the first behavior on one of the index cards to Team 1 and as a team they decide which behavior it is and go to the part of the room designated as either Bully or Bossy. To make it more fun for the students, when they get to the designated part of the room they are to either "moo" like a cow or "snort" like a bull. They are to then explain their answer, and tell how they would handle the situation without getting into trouble if it happened to them. As the facilitator you will need to correct them and guide them in gaining understanding of the difference between these two behaviors, and also to point out that sometimes it is hard to tell the difference. It may depend on how often a certain behavior is targeted to you by one student. Remind the students if they are in doubt if they are being bullied or bossed around they can go to a teacher, counselor, or parent and ask for help.
- Continue reading the cards out to the teams, allowing them to confer and challenge each other if they disagree.

☞ Discussion Questions

- Did your group have trouble determining whether certain behaviors were bossy or bullying behaviors? How did you resolve the disagreement?
- Why is it hard sometimes to tell an adult on a bully?
- Do you think there are more bossy people or more bullies in our school? Why?

☞ Variations

- Prepare your own list of bossy and/or bully behaviors to use, rather than having the students make the lists.
- Have students write their own lists of steps to take if they are being bullied or being bossed around and share with each other. Monitor these lists to keep their options positive and safe.

Lesson 12: Bully or Bossy?

✂ **Activity**

Bossy Cow

Lesson 12: Bully or Bossy?

✂ **Activity**

Bully Bull

Lesson 13: Penny for Your Thoughts

☞ Overview

This lesson gives students the opportunity to put themselves in the shoes of different parties in a bullying situation. They are encouraged to imagine how each person is feeling and what each is thinking. Becoming more aware of others' perspectives can help children handle difficult situations more appropriately.

☞ Grade Level

4th

☞ Materials

- Three copies of "Thinking Bubbles" sheet (found on the next page) for each student
- Pencils or pens
- Pennies for each class member
- "Bully Vignettes" sheet for each student

☞ Time Needed

30 minutes

☞ Objectives

- Students will learn the hand sign for bully.
- Students will be able to recognize the three roles in a bully situation – the victim, the bully, and the bystander.
- Students will develop insights into the thoughts of the three roles.

☞ Procedures

- Teach students the hand sign for bully. Explain to them that in the American Sign Language dictionary the sign for bully is the same as the one for arrogant, big-headed, big shot, and brat. Ask them why they think this is so.

- Ask students if they have ever heard the expression "A penny for your thoughts?" Tell them that today we are going to be talking about the different "thoughts" of the people involved in a bully situation – the bully, the victim, and the bystander(s).
- Distribute three "Thinking Bubbles" sheets to each student. Go over the definitions of each of the roles.
- Give each student a "Bully Vignette" sheet and ask each student to fill in the blanks identifying which person is the victim, which person is the bully, and which person is/are the bystander(s).
- Ask the students to write in their think bubbles what each of the three parties in each situation might be thinking.
- Collect the thinking bubbles and lead a class discussion on the different thoughts and perspectives of the three roles. As the discussion is going on, ask students from time to time if they have heard anything that makes them feel differently about either the victim, the bully, or the bystander.
- Ask students what they could do in each situation to help if one of them were the bystander. Remind them they can always ask a trusted adult for help.
- Obtain permission to take their thinking bubbles worksheets to the 5th grade classes for their lesson.
- Give each student a penny to keep to remember the lesson and how important it is to see everyone's perspective to help you know the best thing to do in a difficult situation.

☞ Discussion Questions

- What is the difference between a target and a victim? Does the target always have to be a victim? Why or why not?
- Would you want someone to tell you if they thought you were acting like a bully? Why or why not?
- Why is it hard to tell on a bully sometimes?

☞ Variations

- Let the students work in small groups, instead of individually.
- Ask students to write their own bully vignettes, and share with the class. Discuss the three roles in these situations.

Lesson 13: Penny for Your Thoughts

✂ Activity

Directions: Give each student three copies of this sheet.
Ask them to number them 1-3.

Victim

Bully

Bystander

✎ BULLY VIGNETTES

PLAYGROUND

Larry is always teased about not being any good at playing soccer. He likes to play, and tries, but can never kick it when it comes to him. No one wants him on their team and every time the teams are picked he is last. In addition to this embarrassment, most days John will yell out, "Nobody wants you on their team. Why don't you just play on the slide or something?" John will try to get all the other kids to join him in laughing at Larry, and telling him to stop trying to play something he is no good at.

Victim is_____ Bully is _____

Bystanders are_____

CLASSROOM

Nancy is a new student who everyone is interested in because she is pretty and smart. One day you come into the room and notice her taking a fancy pen off the teacher's desk and putting it in her pocket. She sees you watching her. Later, during lunch, she tells you in front of three of your friends, that she is starting a special club but that to be in it you have to take something off the teacher's desk and not get caught. She wants all four of you to be in this great club but first you have to steal. Two of your friends say, "Sure, I can do that." You and your other friend just look at each other.

Victim is_____ Bully is _____

Bystanders are_____

FRIEND'S HOUSE

Cindy and Ron, brother and sister, are having a pool party. They invite the whole class to come, but tell you that they hope Fred won't come because he is such a nerd. Fred does come and Cindy and Ron barely speak to him. You notice him sitting alone on the side of the pool and hear Cindy and Ron talking loudly about how some people shouldn't have come if they don't know how to have fun. The only reason they invited the whole class was because their mom made them.

Victim is_____ Bully is _____

Bystanders are_____

Lesson 14: Six Words Only

☞ Overview

This lesson allows interaction between the 4th graders and the 5th graders, giving them the opportunity to understand each other better. The Thinking Bubbles the 4th graders completed in Lesson 13 will be shared with the 5th graders. The 5th graders will then define a bully, a victim, and a bystander in six words only. Their definitions will be shared with the 4th graders.

☞ Grade Level

5th

☞ Materials

- Colorful sentence strips for each student
- Pens or Markers
- "Thinking Bubbles" worksheets from 4th grade lesson
- One copy of "Bully Vignettes" sheet from previous lesson

☞ Time Needed

30 minutes

☞ Objectives

- Students will learn the hand sign for bully.
- Students will listen to thoughts of the 4th graders on bullies, victims, and bystanders.
- Students will write in only six words the definition of a bully, a victim, and a bystander.

☞ Procedures

- Teach students the hand sign for bully. Explain to them that in the American Sign Language Dictionary the sign for bully is the same as the one for arrogant, big-headed, big shot, and brat. Ask them why they think this is so.

- Share with the students the same three vignettes written for the fourth grade, and the thoughts the fourth graders wrote in their think bubbles. Ask students to write definitions of bully, victim, and bystander in only six words on the sentence strips provided. Encourage them to be creative in their definitions. They do not need to write complete sentences
- Read these six word definitions aloud to the class, and discuss insights gained.
- Ask the 5th graders if they would allow you to take their definitions back to the 4th graders to share, to continue overlap between the two grades and increased understanding of the three roles in a bullying situation.

☞ Discussion Questions

- What are the most effective ways you have handled a bully?
- Do you think you can always handle a bullying situation by yourself or do you need to tell a trusted adult sometimes?
- How is talking to an adult about a bully problem different from tattling?
- Why is it hard to talk to an adult about a bully?

☞ Variations

- Let each class choose two students to accompany you to the 4th grade classes with the six word definitions.
- Put the definitions on sentence strips and construct a bulletin board in a prominent place in the school.

Dear Parents,

Today in classroom guidance we learned the sign language for "bully." It is interesting that American Sign Language uses the same sign for this word that it does for "arrogant," "big-headed," "big shot," and "brat!" Our lesson focused on the various roles in a bullying situation: the bully, the target, the victim, and the bystanders. We are hoping to help all our students learn the difference between a bully and someone who is bossy, so that we can empower them to handle some problems independently. That said, however, the bully problem is real in our schools and we also want our students to know how important it is to tell a trusted adult both at school and at home when they are being bullied or see someone else being bullied.

When children help each other by reporting a bullying incident they have observed or been the victim of, they are also empowered and know that it does not have to continue. They can also see that just because someone is a target does not mean they have to be the victim. There are strategies and adults to help.

Ask your child to show you the hand sign for bully and what we talked about in our lesson today. As you make yourself available to hear your child's comments about his or her day you can also help him or her differentiate between bullying and bossy behavior and give ideas for handling both types of situations. Together we can make our school a bully-free zone, a safe and comfortable place for all children to learn and grow.

Sincerely,

Your School Counselor

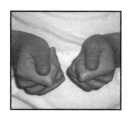

SELF-DISCIPLINE

Self-discipline (control) is a crucial character trait for children to develop to succeed in school and life. When children practice self-discipline at an appropriate developmental level, they gain self-esteem and confidence. Because they normally behave on impulse, children are often not even aware of how much control they actually have over their own bodies. When they realize this, they are empowered to discover they have an active part in their own behavior. Enjoy these lessons as you help children discover and practice this important character trait!

☞ Hand Sign* for this lesson:

SELF   Make a fist with right hand, palm toward chest and thumb sticking up. Starting with hand in front of body, bring hand toward chest.

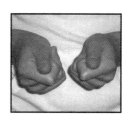

CONTROL   Spread fingers apart and curl fingertips inward on both hands. Put hands against the chest, palms facing in, and bring hands downward with palms facing up.

*Adapted from Costello, Elaine. Concise American Sign Language Dictionary. Random House. 2000.

Lesson 15: I'm In Control of Me!

☞ Overview

Young children often feel that adults control everything they do. This lesson gives them increased awareness of how many actions and movements they are in control of. When we increase this awareness, we help them learn to make better choices in what they do and say.

☞ Grade Level

Pre-Kindergarten

☞ Materials

- Puppet friend

☞ Time Needed

20 minutes

☞ Objectives

- Students will learn the hand sign for self-discipline.
- Students will practice controlling some of their body parts.
- Students will recognize times when controlling their behavior and voice is important.

☞ Procedures

- You and the puppet greet children, and share that your puppet wants to teach them a song. Sing "Head, Shoulders, Knees, and Toes" which also includes the body parts eyes, ears, mouth, and nose. As you sing with them get children active by standing up and pointing to each body part as you sing.
- Ask the puppet if she can make those body parts do what she wants them to do. For example, can she make her head shake? Her shoulders go up and down? Etc. As she does these actions with her body ask children to do the same.

- Ask children, "Well, who is controlling what your parts do?" As they say "I am" tell them "That's right, you are!" You have a lot of control, and as we grow up we need to keep learning how to control what we do and say."
- Give children a few more opportunities to control their body parts by letting them bend knees, wiggle toes, blink eyes, smile, frown, wiggle nose, etc. Ask for ideas from the class so that they can come up with their own ways of making their body do what they want it to do.
- As children are sitting back down and getting settled again ask, "Are there times here in school when you need to control your body so you don't get in time-out? Let's talk about those times."
- Elicit discussion including ideas summarizing with, "During circle time our mouths need to be closed, our ears listening, and our hands still. Let's try this right now."
- Ask the puppet to time the children to see if they can sit this way for a whole minute, which is longer than they might think!
- Teach the hand signs for self-control.

☞ Discussion Questions

- What can you control now that you couldn't when you were a baby?
- How do you feel when you are able to control your voices and actions when you need to?
- Is it always easy to control yourself? What are some times when it is the hardest?

☞ Variations

- Let the children practice sitting still and quiet every day, and increase their time from one minute to two, then three, etc. Let them watch the clock with you so they can see how they are improving and how they can do it even though it is hard.

S E L F - D I S C I P L I N E

Lesson 16: Control Patrol

☞ Overview

Using the metaphor of a referee, this lesson helps young children see the difference between doing just what they want and following certain rules in school. They learn how much control they have over their own behavior, and why it is important to practice using this self-control.

☞ Grade Level

Kindergarten

☞ Materials

- A referee's hat and whistle

☞ Time Needed

20 minutes

☞ Objectives

- Students will learn the hand sign for self-discipline.
- Students will practice following commands given.
- Students will understand the importance of following the rules.

☞ Procedures

- Ask students if they have ever been to a ball game where a referee makes sure everyone follows the rules. Ask students why this is necessary.
- Ask children to tell you some times they have to follow rules in class. Include the following answers: walking in line in the hall, taking turns in centers, not talking unless called on, and putting toys away after playing with them.
- With volunteers role play the above class/school situations with 5 children not using self-discipline. Manage these role plays to keep all children and property safe but allow them to run in the class, grab and go to whatever center they want whenever they want, talk all at once, and leave toys out when finished playing with them. After these role plays ask students, "Well, how does the

© YouthLight Inc.

class look and feel when these students did not use self-discipline and follow the rules? Is it a safe and happy place to be?" Discuss this discovery, and clean up the room before moving on.

- Tell them that today we are going to play a game to see if they can control their actions and follow the rules. Tell them you will be the referee.
- Put on the hat and put the whistle around your neck. Ask the children to stand up. Tell them that when you blow the whistle they are to follow your directions and do just what you say.
- Give the following commands, blowing the whistle between each one: march in place; touch your toes; wrinkle your nose; shout out your name; jump up and down; sing Twinkle, Twinkle, Little Star; raise both arms high; sit back down in your place.
- When children are settled down again, ask them, "Was it hard to follow the directions and do what I asked? Why or why not? "Who controlled what you did? Even though I gave you the direction, you controlled whether or not you followed those directions."
- Teach children the hand sign for self-discipline. Tell them that as they continue to grow up they will be asked to control more and more of their actions and their words. Ask them, "A little while ago we showed what class would be like if no one followed rules and controlled themselves. Even though sometimes we don't want to, we can do it and now we know why it is so important. You can be proud of yourself when you get a smiley face for the day and know that you used your self-discipline and followed the rules."
- Review the hand sign in closing and encourage children to practice their self-discipline every day!

🖙 Discussion Questions

- What are some things adults say to you when you show self-discipline?
- How does this make you feel?
- What are some ways you show self-discipline at home?

🖙 Variations

- Take the students outside to watch a P.E. class playing a game. (This will need to be set up ahead of time with the P. E. teacher.) Ask them to observe how the students are using self-discipline during the game.
- Have children draw pictures of times when they need self-discipline in school or at home.

SELF-DISCIPLINE

Lesson 17: The M&M Challenge*

 Overview

Self-discipline in young children must be practiced to be learned. This lesson gives a fun and tasty way to do that, while also allowing time to process what they learn and apply it to other situations.

 Grade Level

1st

 Materials

- M&Ms®
- Poster with a big green button on it
- Drawing Paper
- Pencils or crayons

 Time Needed

30 minutes

Objectives

- Students will learn the hand sign for self-discipline.
- Students will learn the meaning of self-discipline and practice using it as they play together.
- Students will understand the importance of self-discipline in their lives.

Procedures

- Put 5-10 M&Ms® on each student's desk. Instruct the children not to eat the candy.
- Leave the classroom for a minute to "talk with another teacher," asking the children to wait quietly.
- When you return to the room glance at each student's candy to see if anyone has eaten any of it. Explain that if they were able to wait that is an example of self-discipline, today's lesson.

- Teach the hand sign for self-discipline. Remind them that this is the second sign we have learned that uses the word self, and review self-respect sign.
- Discuss self-discipline with the students asking the following questions: "Who wanted an M&M® badly? How did it feel when the candy was in front of you and there was not an adult around? Were you able to control yourself and not take a piece? If you chose to eat one when you were asked not to how do you feel now?" From this discussion the students will understand that self-discipline is hard, and it takes practice to be able to have it.
- Demonstrate self-talk and how students could use this strategy to do the right thing when it is hard. Ask the students, "What could you think in your head to help you follow the directions not to eat the candy?"
- Ask for a volunteer to pretend to be a robot, and press the big green button on the poster to "activate" the robot. Give simple commands which he follows such as walk, run, sit on floor, laugh, etc. Explain to the children that the student is using his self-discipline to obey the commands.
- Ask the class to help you make a list of when they use self-discipline in the classroom including such times as: wanting to talk, asking a question, lining up, waiting for a turn to get water, working quietly, etc.
- Discuss why self-discipline is important for these daily tasks.
- Give each child a piece of paper and ask them to draw a picture of themselves using self-discipline in class. Make a bulletin board of these pictures titled: "We have self-discipline!"
- Review the hand sign and encourage them to use it to remind themselves of the importance of learning to discipline themselves.

☞ Discussion Questions

- What "self-talk" could you have used to help you not eat the candy?
- What are some ways you kept yourself from eating the candy?
- How did you feel when you were able to wait before you ate the candy?

☞ Variations

- Make a list of students' examples of self-talk and post this list in the classroom for them to refer to when they need help with self-discipline.
- Instead of candy, give them markers and paper, asking them to wait until you come back into the room to use them.

* Copied with permission from Gatewood and Senn. Bee Your Best. Youthlight, 2001.

Lesson 18: A Tower of Trouble

👉 Overview

This lesson uses some favorite storybook characters to help children see the importance of self-discipline in their young lives. The use of blocks as the story is read provides a concrete image of how trouble can grow if we do not take responsibility for our actions. The end of the lesson leaves them with assurance that telling a trusted adult the truth is the way to resolve the problems and get out of trouble.

👉 Grade Level

2nd

👉 Materials

- *The Berenstain Bears' Trouble At School* by Stan and Jan Berenstain
- Small blocks or legos.

👉 Time Needed

30 minutes

👉 Objectives

- Students will learn the hand sign for self-discipline.
- Students will understand how not having self-control can cause continual problems.
- Students will realize that mistakes can be corrected.

👉 Procedures

- Teach students the hand sign, reminding them of the sign for self already learned a few visits ago.
- Lead discussion on meaning of discipline and control.

- Read *The Berenstain Bears' Trouble At School.* Process their understanding by asking the following questions. As the children answer the questions build a block tower with the blocks you brought, adding a block every time the bear makes the situation worse by not using his self-control.
  - What was the first thing Brother Bear did that did not show self-discipline?
  - What did he miss at school while he was out sick?
  - What did he miss at soccer? How did he feel about this when he returned?
  - Why did he do so poorly on the math test?
  - What happened when he got home with the paper to be signed?
  - How did Brother Bear feel during his walk in the forest?
  - What did he do with his test paper while on his walk?
  - Who did Brother tell first about his trouble at school?
  - How did his grandpa help him?
  - How can we get out of a mess we are in so that it doesn't get worse?
  - Where did Mama Bear take him after he told them the truth?
  - Why do you think she did that?
- Point out the tower to the children and summarize with them that one time not using self-discipline can start a series of problems. It is important to remember that we can always stop the problems from getting worse if we use our self-discipline and ask an adult for help, admitting our mistake.
- Go back over the story, stopping at each place when Brother Bear did not use self-discipline. Have children retell the story at each point, showing how everything could have turned out differently if he had used his self-control and done the right thing.
- Review the hand sign for self-discipline and challenge the class to look for ways they can grow every day by being self-disciplined.

☞ Discussion Questions

- What is a "second chance?" Have you ever gotten one after you made a mistake and didn't use your self-control? Tell us about it.
- Why is it hard to have self-discipline? Are some times harder than others? What times?
- Do you sometimes wish you could start over and do something differently? Why?

☞ Variations

- Have students write a letter to Brother Bear giving advice to help him get out of trouble.
- Let each student keep an ongoing list of times they used their self-discipline. This list can be part of their daily writing journals for the next few weeks. Let them share the lists with you next time you are in the classroom.

Lesson 19: Special Delivery of Self- Discipline

☞ Overview

This lesson helps the students see the importance of daily responsibilities in developing self-discipline. They are encouraged to have pride in carrying out these responsibilities and to recognize both the tangible and intangible rewards this self-discipline provides.

☞ Grade Level

3rd

☞ Materials

- *The Paperboy* by Dave Pilkey
- Box of stick-on stars
- A copy of a blank "Self-Discipline Journal" for each student

☞ Time Needed

30 minutes

☞ Objectives

- Students will learn the hand sign for self-discipline.
- Students will identify specific acts they do that show self-discipline.
- Students will understand rewards for developing self-discipline.

☞ Procedures

- Ask students if any of them have jobs or chores they have to do regularly. As you list some on the board, remind students that even though these chores may seem small, they are very important because they are helping them learn self-discipline. Ask them if they always like doing the job or chore they are expected to do? This is self-discipline or self-control, doing what you have to do even when you don't want to. What are some chores in school that you do not always like to do? List some of these on the board as well.

- Teach students the hand sign for self-discipline. Remind them we are reviewing the sign for self that we learned a few visits ago along with respect. Ask them why the word self is important in both these lessons.
- Distribute ten stick-on stars and the Self-Discipline Journal page to each student. Tell them they will be using the stars as they listen to a book you have brought to read to them, *The Paperboy*.
- The book is about a boy about their age who is doing a job that children used to do that adults do now, delivering newspapers. Instruct them to paste a star on one of the spaces provided on their journal page every time they hear something the boy does that would be hard for them to do. At the end of the book ask, "What do you think was the hardest thing he did in the book?"
- The answer here will probably be getting out of bed. Explore this with them, helping them to see how taking the first step in doing something hard is usually the hardest.
- Ask them what rewards the boy received from his paper route.
- Give students time to fill in the page with their own examples of using self-discipline and the rewards they received when they did.
- As time allows let volunteers share their examples and rewards.
- Review the hand sign for self-discipline in closing the lesson.

☞ Discussion Questions

- Would you like to have a job as a paper boy like the boy in the book? Why or why not?
- How do you think the boy felt when he finished his route every day?
- Why do we feel proud when we do a good job at something that is hard? Is feeling proud a good feeling?

☞ Variations

- Ask students to take their self-discipline journals home for homework and have parents add to them if applicable, then sign them.
- Let students interview an adult about their responsibilities when they were growing up, and when they had to use self-discipline.

Lesson 19

✂ Activity

Directions: Put a sticker on a star each time you hear an example of self-discipline in the story. Then fill in the journal page with your own examples of self-discipline and the rewards these behaviors give you.

✎ SELF-DISCIPLINE JOURNAL

TIMES I HAVE SHOWN SELF-DISCIPLINE   REWARDS

1. ....

2. ....

3. ....

4. ....

5. ....

Lesson 20: Will Power is REAL Power

☞ Overview

In this lesson students compare the power of athletic strength to will power. They learn that exercising our will power in school can be just as difficult and powerful as exercising our muscles.

☞ Grade Level

4th

☞ Materials

- 10 pound hand weight
- Construction paper barbell for each student, reproducibles on pages 66 & 67
- Sentence strip which says WILL POWER IS REAL POWER

☞ Time Needed

30 minutes

☞ Objectives

- Students will learn the hand sign for self-discipline.
- Students will identify specific examples of self-discipline on the athletic field and in the classroom.
- Students will make a bulletin board to show examples of their "power" in school.

☞ Procedures

- Hold up the hand weight. Ask the students what this is a symbol of, and elicit the answer "power or strength." Continue the discussion asking, "What does it mean to be powerful? How do people get power? How are people able to lift heavy weights? What happens if they stop this training or exercising? Why do they do it?"
- Ask students if they have ever heard of "will power?" Tell them, "This is the kind of power we all need to be the best we can be, either in school, athletics, music, or anything else. Will power is self-control or self-discipline, the power

to do what we should do. Self-discipline or will power is the power to control your actions and stop doing something harmful and start doing something helpful to your body and your mind. Athletes are always using their will power to help themselves get stronger and faster in their sport. What are some training rules they have to follow that shows their self-discipline?" List some on the board as students answer.

- Ask, "What about their behavior? How do athletes use their will power and self-control to stay in the game?"
- Ask, "How do students use will power and self-discipline in school?" Elicit some responses, list a few on the board, then hand out the paper barbells and ask each student to write at least one thing he or she does that they don't always want to do in their learning that helps them be better learners. Examples may include homework, writing neatly, reading a book you aren't really interested in, redoing a paper that is messy, trying again to understand something that is hard, etc.
- Teach the hand sign for self-discipline. Tell students, "Without will power and self-discipline no athlete would be successful, and without will power and self- discipline no student can be successful either."
- Construct a bulletin board with the sentence strip in the middle and the students' barbells around it.

☞ Discussion Questions

- What does the word power make you think of?
- Are there different kinds of power?
- Do you know someone who is powerful? What makes them powerful?

☞ Variations

- Share with the class a recent news article about a sports player who either showed good self-discipline or no self-discipline and the consequences of the action.
- Assign students to watch TV news and come to class with another example of someone who did or did not show self-discipline and what happened to them.
- Teach the hand sign for powerful to extend the lesson.

☞ Hand Signs* for this powerful:

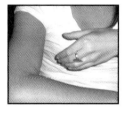

Powerful   Bend left arm in front of your chest. Using right hand in the shape of a C bring the fingertips and thumb down against the biceps of the bent left arm.

*Adapted from Costello, Elaine. Concise American Sign Language Dictionary. Random House. 2000.

Lesson 20: Will Power is REAL Power

✂ Activity

Directions: Write on the barbell something you do in school that shows you have will power.

Lesson 20: Will Power is REAL Power

✂ Activity

Directions: Write on the barbell something you do at home that shows you have will power.

Lesson 21: Voluntary or Involuntary?

 ## Overview

This lesson helps students differentiate between voluntary and involuntary actions. When they realize how many actions they control, they discuss why it is so hard to use our self-discipline at times. Three strong needs are identified, and they are encouraged to accept these needs, but to find positive ways to meet them while maintaining self-discipline in their lives.

 ## Grade Level

5th

 ## Materials

- Examples of automatic gadgets such as a watch, a clock, an electric pencil sharpener, a light bulb, etc.
- A 4" x 6" index card for each student

 ## Time Needed

30 minutes

 ## Objectives

- Students will learn the hand sign for self-discipline.
- Students will learn the difference between voluntary and involuntary actions.
- Students will explore specific roadblocks to self-discipline and ways to overcome them.

Procedures

- Teach the hand sign for self and discipline, reminding students of earlier use of self in the lesson on respect.
- Show them the automated gadgets you have brought asking them what makes these gadgets work. Emphasize the connection of the word "automatic" to "involuntary," and tell them these gadgets work because they are wound up, plugged in, and set to work so we don't have to do anything to them.

- Tell students our amazing human bodies are like that. There are some actions that work without us having to do a thing, and these are called involuntary actions. Start a list of involuntary actions on the board including the following: blinking, swallowing, breathing, and heartbeat.
- Tell students that the other kinds of actions our bodies do are called voluntary. These are the actions we do have control over. List some of these on the board including: talking, walking, stretching, writing, and eating. (Make sure the list for voluntary is longer than the list of involuntary.)
- Point out that sometimes a certain neurological disorder can cause some people not to be able to control certain parts of their bodies the rest of us can and they will develop tics, twitches, etc. that they can not control. We should always be careful not to make fun of such individuals, because what we take for granted as our power to control certain actions they no longer have.
- If we have so much control over our bodies, our mouths, and our actions why is it so hard to control ourselves sometimes?
- Lead a class discussion on why self-discipline is so difficult sometimes.
- Give each student a 4" x 6" index card. Ask them to write in three columns across the top of the card three main reasons why having self-discipline is difficult: My Feelings, My Comfort, My Need to Fit In. Then they are to number 1 to 3 down the side of the card. (A sample card is shown on next page.)
- Give students time to write in five examples of behavior that requires self-discipline and to check which column makes it hard. More than one column can be checked for each behavior. When all are finished group students into small groups of 3-4 and give time to discuss and compare their answers. Ask them to help each other with ways they have overcome the feelings, comfort, and fitting in issues that keep them from using self-discipline.
- Conclude lesson with a class discussion on what they discovered about their difficulties with self-discipline. Review the hand sign for self-discipline.

☞ Discussion Questions

- What is one thing you learned in today's lesson that will help you be more self-disciplined?
- Can you think of any other reasons why self-discipline is hard to achieve sometimes?
- Which one of the three reasons did you check the most often on your card? Why do you think this is so?

☞ Variations

- Ask the students to write an essay on one person who they consider to be very self-disciplined.
- Have the students interview their parents, asking them how they need self-discipline in their lives and how it has helped them.
- Make copies of the sample card on card stock instead of having students create their own.

Lesson 21: Voluntary or Involuntary?

✂ Activity

Directions: Write four behaviors that require self-discipline and check one or more columns that explain why this behavior is hard for you to do at school.

OBSTACLES TO SELF-DISCIPLINE

Behaviors That Require Self-Discipline	My Feelings	My Comfort	My Need To Fit In
1. Being quiet in class			X
2.			
3.			
4.			
5.			

OBSTACLES TO SELF-DISCIPLINE

✂ Activity

Directions: Write four behaviors that require self-discipline and check one or more columns that explain why this behavior is hard for you to do at home.

OBSTACLES TO SELF-DISCIPLINE			
Behaviors That Require Self-Discipline	**My Feelings**	**My Comfort**	**My Need To Fit In**
1. Getting out of bed		X	
2.			
3.			
4.			
5.			

Dear Parents,

Self-Discipline! Such a big word for children. In my experience as a school counselor, I have learned that children enjoy learning big words. They are also proud when they can display a character trait that is difficult to obtain, but which helps them all day long in their interactions with others.

Because children are naturally impulsive, self-discipline is a difficult trait to develop. One of the challenges in teaching this trait is to understand the developmental level of our children so that we remain realistic in our expectations. When they master appropriate self-discipline they discover that they have an active role in their own behavior, and it can become an exciting challenge to them. Children do not enjoy being punished and disciplined due to lack of self-discipline, so when taught in an interesting, fun way self-discipline can be a friend to them in their active, energetic, busy lives.

Encourage your child to show you the hand sign for self-discipline and ask him or her about our lesson today. Look for ways at home to help them develop this trait by expecting them to practice patience, waiting, following directions, and thinking of others as well as themselves. We can share their pride as we see them making progress in this important quality – self-discipline.

Sincerely,

Your School Counselor

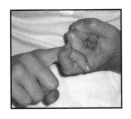

FRIENDSHIP

There are many lessons children can learn to help them be better friends. Sometimes sharing, thinking of others, and empathy do not come easily, but with careful understanding and developmentally appropriate expectations all children can learn and practice what it means to be a good friend. The rewards children receive when they possess these valuable skills are vital for their emotional well being the rest of their lives. The following lessons focus on specific actions and thought patterns that pave the way for being and having good friends.

☞ Hand Sign* for this lesson:

FRIEND   Bend the right index finger, palm facing down, and hook it over the left index finger, palm facing up. Then repeat, putting the left palm facing down and the right palm facing up.

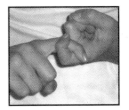

*Adapted from Costello, Elaine. Concise American Sign Language Dictionary. Random House. 2000.

Lesson 22: We Care and We Share!

 ## Overview

This lesson gives young children opportunities for developing positive and friendly behaviors toward each other. Friendship skills must be learned at this age, and with the help of a friendly puppet and role playing, children practice these important skills.

 ## Grade Level

Pre-K

 ## Materials

- Puppet
- Basket of toys such as blocks, a doll, a ball, a book, and markers.
- Clear jar and supply of pom poms

 ## Time Needed

20 minutes

 ## Objectives

- Students will learn the hand sign for friend.
- Students will identify friendly acts they can do for each other every day.
- Students will explore the difference between sharing and taking turns.

Procedures

- Begin lesson with the puppet telling you how sad she is because her friend will not play with her today. When you ask her why she tells you because she would not let her have a turn with the soccer ball.
- Ask children if they know why the friend did not want to play with her.
- Encourage them to tell the puppet how she could have played in a more friendly way by sharing or taking turns with the ball.

- Bring out the toys you have brought and allow volunteers to role play ways they can take turns or share the items. Point out that some items can be shared and used at the same time, and it works better with other toys if we take turns.
- Put them in small groups of four and let each group show how to either share or take turns with: a pile of blocks; one doll; one ball; one book; and 5 markers.
- Tell them that you are going to leave a clear jar and a plastic bag full of pom poms with the teacher. When she sees someone in the class either sharing or taking turns with a friend, she will put a pom pom in the jar. When the jar has 25 pom poms she will tell the counselor, and the counselor will reward the whole class by taking them on an extra 10 minute play time at a time that suits both the teacher and the counselor.
- Teach the hand sign for friend, and practice doing it together.

☞ Discussion Questions

- What is a friendly act someone did for you so far today?
- What is a friendly act you did for someone today?
- How do you feel when someone is friendly to you?

☞ Variations

- Ask a child to pick an object or toy from the room and bring it to you. Ask the class, "Is this something you would share or is it something you would need to take turns with?" Give them a few other opportunities to answer this question about different toys in the room.
- Bring puppet back out and let him/her tell the class how much better she/he feels now that her friend has learned to share and take turns.

Lesson 23: Friendship Chain Reaction

 Overview

This lesson demonstrates to children in a concrete way how one friendly action can cause another and so on. They are given the challenge to practice friendly behaviors in the class and watch their paper clip chain grow as the teacher observes these acts.

Grade Level

Kindergarten

Materials

- Large multi-colored paper clips

Time Needed

20 minutes

Objectives

- Students will learn the hand sign for friend.
- Students will identify friendship behaviors they can do every day.
- Students will understand how one friendly act can start another, etc.

Procedures

- Let students watch you string two paper clips together. Attach these first two clips to the ceiling or a high place in the classroom. Tell the children that the class is going to make a Friendship Chain and we want it to go all the way to the floor.
- Teach students the hand sign for friend. Lead a short discussion about what a friend is and isn't. Focus on specific and concrete acts friends do for each other like sharing, helping carry something, getting the teacher if someone is hurt, letting others have a turn, smiling, letting someone join your game, etc.

- Show them how one kind act will produce a "reaction" and another kind act may follow, etc. You can do this with puppets or enact a role play with student volunteers. Tell them this is called a chain reaction.
- Also demonstrate how chain reactions can go the other way, and show what happens if someone is mean or rude to a friend. Then the friend may do something mean or rude to someone else and the actions that result are not a pleasant chain reaction.
- Explain that the teacher is going to add paper clips to the chain as she sees friendship acts in the class. Challenge the class to get their chain all the way to the floor by the end of the week.
- In closing the lesson, review the hand sign for friend.

☞ Discussion Questions

- Can you think of a friendly act you have done for someone today?
- Where are some other places besides school where we can do friendly acts for others?
- Why are friends important?

☞ Variations

- The counselor can observe the class for a few minutes during lunch or recess and add a link or two that he/she can tell the children about at the next class visit.
- The students could set a goal for their class to see how many days it takes to get their chain to the floor.

Lesson 24: Need a Friend Today?

 **Overview**

This lesson leads children to give friendship a reality check. They are helped to see that no friend is perfect, including themselves, and that relationships are a give and take, but worth the patience and time involved.

Grade Level

1st

Materials

- *Trouble With Friends* by Stan and Jan Berenstain
- Puppet friend

Time Needed

30 minutes

Objectives

- Students will learn the hand sign for friend.
- Students will be able to say three reasons we need friends.
- Students will understand neither ourselves nor our friends are perfect.

Procedures

- Counselor and puppet have the following conversation:
  Counselor: Hi, Maryann. You look happy today, is there a special reason?
  Puppet: Yes, my friend is coming home with me after school to play all afternoon.
  C: That does sound like fun. Friends are important to have, aren't they?
  P: Yes, because sometimes I get bored at home by myself. Having someone else around makes all my toys more fun to play with.
  C: What else is special about your friend?
  P: I can tell she cares about me, and if I am sad or sick she is sorry and wants me to feel better.

C: She sounds like a great friend. Do you ever have any trouble when you are together?

P: Well, yes. Sometimes we argue about what to play and whose turn it is, and we get mad at each other. Is that OK?

C: Well, Maryann, all friends get grumpy sometimes, and we have to forgive each other and understand that even the best friend isn't perfect, and neither are we.

P: Do we have a book to share with the children about this?

C: Yes, we do. Let's read it together now.

- Counselor reads *Trouble With Friends*. After reading, process with the following questions:
  - Why was sister so happy when Lizzy moved in?
  - What were some of the activities they liked to do together?
  - What kind of trouble did they have when they were playing school? (bossy and braggy)
  - Why did Sister take her dolls and go home?
  - How did she feel when she did this? How did Lizzy feel?
  - What are some activities we need friends to do with us that we can't do alone?
  - What did Sister's mom tell her she could do all by herself? (be lonesome)
  - How did Sister and Lizzy solve the problem? (Lizzy was thoughtful to return the teddy bear and Sister suggested taking turns.)

- Teach students the hand sign for friend. Ask them, "If one hand is you and one is your friend why do you think we turn our hands over when we do this sign?" Help them see that this means that sometimes our friend is "on top" and gets what he/she wants and sometimes we are "on top" and get what we want.

- Close lesson with each child shaking the hand of a neighbor and saying, "I am glad you are my friend."

👉 Discussion Questions

- Do you have a friend in your neighborhood like Lizzy?
- What happens when you and your friend don't want to play the same thing?
- How do you solve the problem when you and your friend argue?

👉 Variations

- Put together a class list of activities that can be done alone and activities you must have a friend to do with you. Discuss how important friends are and why we need them.

Lesson 25: One Potato, Two Potato

 Overview

This is a lesson which provides interaction between the younger and the older students in your school. After a lesson on the similarities and needs of all of us, and acknowledging that we all have friendship problems from time to time, the second graders compile a list of questions about friendship for the fifth graders to answer.

 Grade Level

2nd

 Materials

- Bag of five potatoes
- Potato peeler
- Overhead with blank transparency, class whiteboard, or computer

 Time Needed

30 minutes

 Objectives

- Students will learn the hand sign for friend.
- Students will understand that friends are unique on the outside but a lot alike on the inside.
- Students will write friendship questions to fifth graders.

 Procedures

- Teach the hand sign for friend. Discuss the meaning of how the sign is done.
- Ask five students to pick a potato and study it for a few minutes. When each student has studied "his" or "her" potato put them back in the container and mix them up. Take out one potato at a time and ask whose it is. Most students will be able to recognize their potato. Ask them why. Explain the differences each potato has on the outside - color, size, shape, markings, etc. that makes that potato unique. Ask children how this relates to our friends.

- Peel two potatoes and ask the students how they are different on the inside. Most will say they are not, and they can no longer recognize "their" potato. Ask how this relates to our friends. Encourage discussion of how most of us are very much alike on the inside. Ask students to tell you some ways we are all alike on the inside and list on board. Include: we want others to be nice to us, to treat us fairly, and to let us play with them.
- Tell the class we are going to let some of the older students in the school help us with some of our friendship problems. Since we all have problems from time to time, we can use the older students' help.
- On the overhead, the board, or computer, write the questions the students would like you to take to the older students to answer. Some examples are:
  - What do you do when you are so mad at a friend that you yell at them and tell them you are not ever going to be their friend again?
  - How many friends should I have?
  - Can I be friends with a student in another grade if we have fun together?
  - What if I don't like to do the same things one of my friends does anymore?
  - Should I always want to play with my best friend?
  - What if someone invites my best friend to play and I am not invited?
  - Do you ever get jealous when your friend is playing with someone else?
  - What do you do?
- When you have about 10 questions tell the students that you will take them to the fifth graders to get some answers. You will bring the answers back in a few days. In the meantime, keep thinking about the importance of friends and keep trying to be the best friend you can be, not a perfect one just a good one!
- Close by reviewing the hand sign for friend.

☞ Discussion Questions

- How would you describe a good friend?
- In what ways are you a good friend?
- Why are friends important?
- Does everyone have problems with friends sometimes?

☞ Variations

- Have the class choose two representatives to go with you to take the questions to the fifth graders.
- You could use apples or oranges in this lesson and then pass around sections for the children to enjoy after you have peeled them.

Lesson 26: Building Bridges

 Overview

This lesson uses the metaphor of a bridge to illustrate to the children the power of friendship. The use of music also captures their imaginations and helps anchor the importance of connecting with each other.

Grade Level

3rd

Materials

- *Love Can Build A Bridge* by Naomi Judd (This book can be bought with an accompanying tape or CD of the song by the same name.)
- Pictures of either local or famous bridges or both (examples: Golden Gate Bridge, London Bridge, Brooklyn Bridge, etc.)

Time Needed

30 minutes

Objectives

- Students will learn the hand sign for friend.
- Students will understand the metaphor of building a bridge to friendships.
- Students will identify specific actions they can do to build bridges between themselves and others.

Procedures

- Teach the hand sign for friend. Discuss the significance of turning hands over as you do the sign.
- Lead a short discussion about bridges. Put up the pictures of bridges you have brought as you discuss. Include the following questions:
    - What does a bridge do? What are they for?
    - What are some bridges you have crossed over either in the car or on foot?

- Do you know the names of the bridges I have pictures of? (Identify them.)
- What would happen if a bridge was not built over a body of water or a divide in the land?
- Tell students we are going to listen to a song today about building a different kind of bridge. As we listen we will be looking at a book that has pictures to go with the words. Ask students to listen carefully and to look carefully at the pictures as they listen.
- Play the tape or CD and let the song tell the story. Turn the pages of the book slowly, in sync with the words of the song.
- When the book and song are finished ask the children if anyone noticed anything interesting about the different children in the book. You want them to realize that the children are of all ages and sizes, and that each page has one child helping another. On the very next page the child who was helped is now the helper. Go back through the pages and let all the children see this.
- On the last page all the children are holding hands. Stop on this picture and ask the children if this reminds them of anything. Reinforce that this is a picture of a bridge of people who are held together by helpful and caring acts, the kind of acts friends do for each other.
- Ask them for examples of the acts the children did in the book. Were they hard to do? Did they cost any money? Did they hurt? As all the answers to these questions are, "No," challenge the students to continue to do these acts for others every day, as we build our own bridge to friendship here in this class and in this school.
- Review the hand sign for friend and do it together as you close the lesson.

☞ Discussion Questions

- How did you feel as you listened to the song and looked at the pictures?
- Why are bridges important? Why are friends important? How are they alike?
- What is the nicest act a friend has done for you today?

☞ Variations

- Play the song and look through the book a second time, letting the children sing along.
- Leave the book in the classroom for a few days so that the children can look at the pictures individually and think about the kinds of friendly acts they see.

Lesson 27: Am I Being Fair?

 ## Overview

Children can have unreasonable and unfair expectations of their friends, and this leads to disappointments and arguments. This lesson helps the students see that unrealistic expectations can be turned into realistic ones, and it shows them how to do this.

 ## Grade Level

4th

Materials

- Copy of "Our Expectations of Our Friends" worksheets on the following pages for each student

Time Needed

30 minutes

 ## Objectives

- Students will learn the hand sign for friend.
- Students will understand the difference between fair and unfair expectations of our friends.
- Students will identify unfair expectations they have for their friends.

Procedures

- Teach the hand sign for friend. Encourage discussion on the meaning of the hands changing positions.
- Write "Fair," "Unfair," and "Expectations" on the board, and discuss the meanings of these words.
- Tell the students that today we are going to talk about just what is fair to expect from our friends and what is unfair. Ask them if they have any ideas before you give them the accompanying worksheet.

- Give out the worksheet on the next page. Ask the students to complete the top half of the page by putting a "U" beside each expectation we may have of our friends that is Unfair and an "F" beside each that is Fair. Give them a few minutes to complete this independently, then let them share with a classmate. When all have shared in groups of two or three, conduct a whole class discussion.
- As they discuss encourage them to think about what unfair expectations they have had in the past of their friends. What happens to the relationship when we have too many unfair expectations?
- Ask them to fill in the bottom section of the page with other expectations they may have of their friends. Indicate if they think they are Fair or Unfair. Mark each accordingly. If the students need help you may suggest the following:
  - My friends should play at my house every day.
  - My friends always wait for me everywhere I go.
  - My friends have to help me all the time.
  - My friends have to sit by me only.
  - My friends should listen to me.
  - My friends should like the same music I like.
  - My friends should take turns with me in a game.
- Discuss the responses to this half of the page, pointing out that the words "always," "have to," and "only" turn fair expectations into unfair ones.
- Ask the class to choose one unfair expectation they identified today, and for the next week remember it is unfair and change their thinking about it. Tell them you are interested in hearing what happens, and will be asking them as you see them. (Remember to check with some students to reinforce this assignment.)
- Close the lesson with the review of the hand sign for friend.

☞ Discussion Questions

- Did you discover some unrealistic expectations you have of your friends in today's lesson?
- How can you change your thinking about these expectations and be fairer to your friend?
- What could you say to a friend to help him/her see that he/she has unfair expectations of you?

☞ Variations

- Join the children on the playground the following week. Observe their play, listen to their arguments, and help them apply today's lesson to their actual friendship problems and challenges.
- Ask children to write a letter to a friend, telling them how much they appreciate their friendship.

✏ Lesson 27: Am I Being Fair?

OUR EXPECTATIONS OF OUR FRIENDS
FAIR OR UNFAIR?

The following are some expectations we may have of our friends. Put an "F" beside the ones you think are Fair and a "U" beside the ones you think are Unfair.

_____1. Friends should always be in a good mood.

_____2. All my friends have to play with me everyday.

_____3. Friends treat each other with respect.

_____4. Friends play with different people some days.

_____5. My friends have to smile at me every time they see me.

_____6. My friends should always pay attention to me when I am around.

✎ Lesson 27: Am I Being Fair?

OUR EXPECTATIONS OF OUR FRIENDS

FAIR OR UNFAIR?

List some expectations you have for your friends and indicate if you think they are Unfair or Fair.

_____ **1.** ....

_____ **2.** ....

_____ **3.** ....

_____ **4.** ....

_____ **5.** ....

_____ **6.** ....

Lesson 28: Friendship Q and A

☞ Overview

This lesson gives the older students a chance to look at the rewards and challenges of being a friend, while at the same time helping younger students with their questions about friendship. This give and take, learning and teaching cycle, is a dynamic way to teach the qualities of being a good friend.

☞ Grade Level

5th

☞ Materials

- Questions on friendship from the 2nd grade lesson
- Copy of "Traits of a Friend" worksheet on page 90 for each student
- Copy of "FriendAcrostic" worksheet on page 91 for each student

☞ Time Needed

30 minutes

☞ Objectives

- Students will learn the hand sign for friend.
- Students will prioritize the top 10 friendship qualities.
- Students will write answers to friendship questions to second graders.

☞ Procedures

- Teach the hand sign for friend to students. Discuss the meaning of the hands changing position, and how this relates to friendship.
- Give students the following list of personality traits, and ask them to pick out the ten most important qualities they look for in a friend.
- Ask for volunteers to read their lists, and discuss that no two lists will be the same. Ask, "Why is that? Don't we all want the same thing in a friend? Can one friend be all these things for us? Why or why not?"

- Ask the students if they ever have problems with their friends. Do they think their problems are the same or different than they were when they were in 2nd grade?
- Tell them that today you need their help in assisting our school's second graders. Since they are older and know more, maybe they can help the younger students with their friendship problems. Say, "I am going to read ten friendship problems the second graders gave me, and ask you to answer them as to how they should handle this problem. I will read all your answers and choose some to share with the second graders at my next class visit. I will also bring your answers back and read some of them to you at another visit, so that you can learn from each other as well. If you do not want your answers read out loud to your classmates, just write that on your paper and I will not use your answers."
- Read each of the second graders questions aloud to the class and give them time to answer. Take up all the papers and close the lesson with a review of the hand sign for friend.

☞ Discussion Questions

- Would you add any friendship traits to the list we used? What would you add?
- Were you surprised at some of the questions from the 2nd graders? Which ones?
- Were any of the questions hard to answer? Which ones?

☞ Variations

- Take two classroom representatives with you to the 2nd grade classes to help you give the answers to the questions posed.
- Ask the fifth graders to write paragraphs about what they have learned about friendship since 2nd grade to share with the younger students.

✎ Lesson 28: Friendship Q and A

Directions: Check the ten most important qualities you value in a friend.

TRAITS OF A FRIEND

❑ Loyal

❑ Honest

❑ Neat

❑ Fair

❑ Patient

❑ Energetic

❑ Polite

❑ Pretty or Handsome

❑ Popular

❑ Smart

❑ Sensitive

❑ Forgiving

❑ Brave

❑ Funny

❑ Happy

❑ Generous

❑ Gentle

❑ Kind

❑ Talented

❑ Friendly

❑ Helpful

❑ Respectful

❑ Positive

✎ Lesson 28: Friend Acrostic

Directions: Describe your friend by using each letter in the word "FRIEND."

F _____

R _____

I _____

E _____

N _____

D _____

Dear Parents,

Today in your child's classroom guidance lesson we learned the sign language hand signal for friend. Our lesson centered around the importance of friends, what encourages and/or discourages others from wanting to be our friends, and how we are all very similar in our needs for friendship.

During the elementary years our children are learning valuable lessons every day about the challenges of being a friend and having friends. They need our support, understanding, and sometimes gentle prodding as they develop these very important relationships. Our task as significant adults in their lives is to provide them opportunities for play dates outside of school, membership in teams or groups where they learn the valuable lessons of cooperation and competition, and the invaluable gift of our time to listen to them as they work through their friendship problems. We need to model the importance of friends in our own lives so that they will learn that, even with occasional problems and disagreements, friendships are important and worth the work.

We can also enjoy with them the fun friends bring to our lives, and how much happier we all are when we have people we can talk to, play with, and laugh with. Have fun helping your children have fun with their friends!

Sincerely,

Your School Counselor

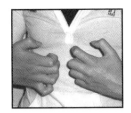

ANGER MANAGEMENT

Helping children from a very early age identify and manage their anger is a crucial task if they are going to grow up emotionally well-adjusted. This is challenging, because young children are not developmentally ready to articulate their feelings. Caring adults can help children learn to identify both the feeling of anger and some concrete strategies they can use to manage it so that they can calm down and think. As with all the sections of the book, these lessons meet the children where they are developmentally, so that by the 5th grade the students are identifying degrees of anger and how to cope throughout the spectrum. All children need to be told many times that anger is a normal human emotion. What we do with our anger is the important part, and there are many strategies to try as we grow and learn.

☞ Hand Signs* for this lesson:

<u>ANGER</u>   Hold both hands in front of you at your lower chest, with the fingertips of both hands curled inward. Bring hands upward and apart, ending at the shoulders.

<u>CONTROL</u> Spread fingers apart and curl fingertips inward on both hands. Put hands against the chest, palms facing in, and bring hands downward with palms facing up and hands in a fist.

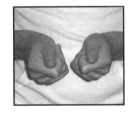

(Remind students that we have already learned sign in the Self-Discipline/Self Control lesson)

*Adapted from Costello, Elaine. Concise American Sign Language Dictionary. Random House. 2000.

Lesson 29: Just Say Grrrr.....

 Overview

Anger can be a scary emotion for young children. This lesson helps them see that it is a feeling we all have, even normally happy puppets, and that there are some things we can do to help ourselves feel better.

 Grade Level

Pre-K

 Materials

- Puppet friend

 Time Needed

20 minutes

 Objectives

- Students will learn the hand sign for anger control.
- Students will share ideas of what makes them angry.
- Students will practice movements and sounds to calm themselves down.

 Procedures

- Begin lesson by telling children that Maryann (puppet's name) is very angry today and is in a bad mood. Let Maryann grumble under her breath and not greet the class as she usually does.
- When children ask why she is mad tell them her mother would not let her watch TV this morning when she wanted to. Ask them if they have ever gotten angry at their parents. As hands go up, let different students share what makes them angry, either at home or at school.
- Ask the puppet what she did when she got mad at her mother. The puppet answers that she slammed the door and yelled. Ask her if that made her feel better and she tells you no, and that it got her in worse trouble.

- Ask the children what they do when they are mad. Tell them that today we are going to practice making some sounds and doing some movements that may make us feel better so we don't get in trouble when we are angry.
- Teach children the hand sign for anger control. Tell them everyone gets angry and that is normal, but as we grow up we begin to learn how to be mad without getting in trouble.
- Using an example they gave you for something that makes them mad, like being told it is time to get ready for bed when they are playing, show the students that they can take deep breaths, count to 10, and just say grrr…
- Let them practice saying grrr and stomping their feet, running in place, moving arms around, or other motions that engage their muscles and get them active. Explain to them that these motions and sounds can help us get the mad out.
- Role play some additional scenarios that would make children mad that happen to them either at home or school. As they suggest situations, let them practice stomping, running in place, and saying grrr. If they start laughing tell them this is another good way to get the mad out, find something funny and start laughing until you feel better.
- Review the hand sign for anger control.

☞ Discussion Questions

- How does your face look when you are angry?
- Does everyone get angry sometimes?
- Do you sometimes get into trouble at home or at school when you are angry?

☞ Variations

- Play music that the children can stomp and march to as they say grrrr..
- Designate a special place in the classroom where children can go when they are angry to calm down.

Lesson 30: Thunder and Lightning

 Overview

This lesson helps students understand that situations arise all day that could cause us to feel angry, and there are many ways to handle these situations so that we feel better. The story of Cumulus who turns into a storm cloud when angry gives them a metaphor for the harm anger can cause and ideas for handling it positively and constructively.

 Grade Level

Kindergarten

 Materials

- Two sets of rhythm band cymbals and two drums

 Time Needed

20 minutes

 Objectives

- Students will learn the hand sign for anger control.
- Students will identify situations that make them angry.
- Students will learn positive ways to calm themselves down.

Procedures

- Ask children if they know what anger is. Have a short discussion about the feeling of anger, and how it is sometimes called "mad," but they mean the same thing. Ask them if they have ever done anything when they were mad that they wish they hadn't done later when they calmed down.
- Explain that when they do or say something they don't really mean they have let their angry feeling take control. Remind them of the self-control lesson and how we can continue to learn to control ourselves and our feelings. Tell them that today we are going to meet a little cloud named Cumulus who learns to control his temper.
- Teach the hand sign for anger control.

- Give out the cymbals and drums to four students, making sure the others know everyone will get a turn. Tell the story of Cumulus on the following page. When Cumulus begins to get angry have the drummers pound on the drum (thunder) and when he loses control have the cymbals crash (lightning).
- When the story is finished ask the children: What made Cumulus angry? What happened when he got angry? Did this make him feel better? What are some things his mother told him he could do to keep from turning into cumulonimbus, the storm cloud? Have you ever tried any of these ideas yourself?
- Read the following situations and give each child a turn with either the cymbals or the drums as you role play what they might want to do when they get angry. Then role play an action that would be helpful, such as one of the ones Cumulus' mother suggested. Ask the children which actions would help the situation and which would make it worse.

  Anger situations:
  - Your little brother has gone into your room again and all your toys are on the floor.
  - Your friend would not give you a turn on the swing and now recess is over.
  - Someone on the bus calls you a name.
  - Your mother tells you it is time for bed, and you are in the middle of a good TV show.
  - The teacher tells you to go to time out because you yelled at someone.
  - You want to tell your daddy about the movie, but your sister is doing all the talking and won't give you a turn.
  - It is your turn to sit in the front seat, but your brother gets there first and your mom does not make him move.
  - The cafeteria runs out of chocolate milk, and you don't like white milk.
  - You were not talking, but someone else at the table was and you got fussed at for it.
  - The teacher won't call on you and you want a turn to talk right now.
- Review the hand sign for anger control, and remind the children not to cause a thunderstorm the next time they get mad.

☞ Discussion Questions

- Have you ever noticed the clouds and how different they look at different times?
- Who are some people you can go to when you are angry who could make you feel better?
- Do you have a favorite thing to do to calm down when you are angry?

☞ Variations

- Use a hand chime, in contrast to the cymbal, when children present a good idea for an anger situation.
- Take children outside to lie on the grass and look at the clouds as you tell them the story of Cumulus.

CUMULUS THE CLOUD GETS
ANGRY*

O nce there was a little white cloud named Cumulus. He loved to float all over the sky and watch little boys and girls playing down below. One day he was floating along and a bigger cloud just flew by and bumped right into him. It didn't really hurt, but it made him mad because the big cloud did not ever say he was sorry!

Cumulus began getting madder and madder just thinking about it, and he realized he was heading for trouble. For you see, when Cumulus got really angry he turned into Cumulonimbus, the thundercloud. When this happened he got very loud and scary, and sometimes he even caused people to get wet. One time when he was very mad and made a loud thunder noise he saw a cute little puppy run for cover, and knew he had scared him. Cumulus didn't like to scare people and animals, but he just got so mad.

He decided he needed to ask for help so he went to find his mother. She was close by and had been watching what was happening. She told him, "Cumulus, you are not hurt are you?" Cumulus answered, "No, I am not hurt, just mad." "Well," his mom answered, "It is OK to be mad, but let's practice some ways to get the mad out that won't cause a terrible storm this time."

So Cumulus and his mom talked about it and came up with some good ideas that you and I can do too, when we get angry. We can:

- Count to 10
- Take deep breaths
- Walk (or blow) away
- Listen to music
- Read a book
- Draw a picture
- Talk to someone we trust, like a parent or teacher or counselor
- Exercise (run, kick a ball, ride a bike, etc.)
- Talk to ourselves and tell ourselves to calm down

After Cumulus and his mom had their talk this is what he did. He told himself he was not hurt, and he didn't want to cause all the people down below any more trouble so he would just blow around a lot until he was tired. When he did this, he realized it did take a lot of the mad out, and he forgot about the bigger cloud who had bumped him. He enjoyed the rest of his day, playing and flying high.

If you watch the clouds today, maybe you will see Cumulus learning how to control his anger, just like you can too!

Adapted from Gatewood, Betts. Counseling by PowerPoint. Youthlight, Inc. 2005.

Lesson 31: Let's Cool It

 ## Overview

This lesson assures children that anger is a normal feeling, but one which can cause us trouble if we do not control it. Role playing various strategies lets them practice positive ways to control this powerful emotion.

 ## Grade Level

1st

 ## Materials

- Balloon
- *If You're Angry and You Know It* by Cecily Kaiser

 ## Time Needed

30 minutes

 ## Objectives

- Students will learn the hand signs for anger control.
- Students will explore reasons they get angry.
- Students will identify three non-harmful ways to let their anger out.

Procedures

- Teach students the hand sign for anger control.
- Ask them for some reasons why they get mad and list a few on the board.
- As they are giving their reasons, you are blowing up the balloon a little more with each reason. When the balloon is fully inflated ask them what would happen if you kept blowing into it. They will tell you it will pop. Explain to students that this is what can happen to us if we don't "get the mad out." We don't pop exactly but we lose our tempers and yell, hit, or do something that is dangerous or hurtful to someone else.
- Tell them that everyone gets angry sometimes, and there are ways to cool down that lets the air out of our balloon before we pop! For fun turn the balloon loose at this point and let the children watch it fly around the room!

- Read *If You're Angry and You Know It!*
- Ask children to pay attention to the things that happen to make the children in the story angry and what they do to calm down.
- After reading the book, have the children stand in two groups on either side of the room. As you go through the book again one side will act out what makes the child mad and the other side will do the strategy. The different scenarios will be:
  - A boy drops his book bag.   **He stomps his feet.**
  - Someone pulls a girl's hair.   **She bangs a drum in music class.**
  - Someone sticks her tongue out at a boy.   **He walks away.**
  - Mud splashes on a girl's dress.   **She takes deep breaths.**
  - A boy's block tower falls down.   **He tells a friend what happened.**
- After role playing the first time do it again letting the different sides switch so that each child has had a turn to act out the actions that make us mad and a good strategy for helping us to feel better.
- Encourage the children to use these strategies every day, and close by reviewing the hand sign for anger control.

☞ Discussion Questions

- Have any of the things that happened to the children in the book ever happened to you?
- How did you show your anger?
- What is your favorite new idea of something to do the next time you get angry?

☞ Variations

- Instead of reading the book, sing it to the tune of the old favorite, "If You're Happy and You Know It."
- Give each child a picture of a balloon and ask them to draw themselves inside the balloon doing something that will make them feel better the next time they are angry.

Lesson 32: From Stormy to Fluffy

👉 Overview

This lesson gives students the opportunity to turn dark angry thoughts and feelings into light, calmer ones. They are also made aware of how their faces and bodies change when they are mad, and how they can regain their calmer feelings through a variety of positive strategies.

👉 Grade Level

2nd

👉 Materials

- Construction paper dark storm clouds for each student copied from the following reproducible page
- Construction paper clouds copied from reproducible on following page (You can put a few cotton balls on each cloud to add to the soft effect.)
- An empty bulletin board or space on the class whiteboard or chalk board

👉 Time Needed

30 minutes

👉 Objectives

- Students will learn the hand sign for anger control.
- Students will draw a self-portrait of their face when angry.
- Students will identify positive ways to deal with their anger.

👉 Procedures

- Lead a short discussion on anger, showing students your face when you are mad. Make sure they notice your eyes, eyebrows, mouth, jaw line, etc. and that they recognize the tightness in your face.
- Ask a few students to share things that make them angry and write on the board as they talk. Help all children to understand that anger is not a bad feeling, but it is one we need to learn to control so we don't get in trouble by saying or doing something mean. Teach the hand sign for anger control.

- Distribute the dark storm clouds, and ask each student to draw his or her face on the cloud. Tell them to make their face as mad as they can, paying attention to specific parts of their face like eyes, eyebrows, jaw, mouth, etc.
- As the children are drawing, circulate around room commenting and helping those who need it. Ask each child to put his or her name on their drawing.
- Ask the children for some ideas of what we can do to calm down when we are mad. Bring out the soft white paper clouds and write a different strategy on each cloud as they give you ideas. Include the following:
  - Take deep breaths
  - Count to 20
  - Talk about it to someone you trust.
  - Run, walk, ride your bike or do something outside.
  - Draw a picture.
  - Have some alone time in your room.
  - Listen to music.
  - Talk to yourself saying things like, "I can get over this, I just need to calm down." Or "It's ok to be angry, and I will feel better in a few minutes."
  - Call a friend.
  - Get help from an adult.
  - Read a book.
- With the children's help construct a class bulletin board with the mad storm cloud faces in a column on one side and the cloud strategies in a column on the other. Ask each student to choose one or two things they like to do to calm down and let them draw a line from their face to the strategy they like to use.
- After each child has had a turn, lead a discussion on how many ways there are to help ourselves feel better when we are mad. Encourage them to look at this board to remind themselves of what they can do.
- Close with a review of today hand sign for anger control.

☞ Discussion Questions

- What do you notice about our eyes in our mad pictures? Our mouths? Our eyebrows?
- How are these same features on our faces different when we are not angry?
- Which way do you prefer your face to be?

☞ Variations

- Give a homework assignment for the children to ask their parents what they do when they are angry. Share these lists with the class.
- Add a happy face cloud to the board any time you see a student using one of the anger control strategies.

✎ Lesson 32: From Stormy to Fluffy

✂ Activity

Directions: Copy and cut out a storm cloud for each student

✎ Lesson 32: From Stormy to Fluffy

✂ Activity

Directions: Copy and cut out a white fluffy cloud for each student

Lesson 33: I'm Talking to Me!

 Overview

This lesson introduces children to the idea of "self-talk," a powerful tool for controlling one's emotions. They leave the lesson with their favorite self-talk messages written down for them to use the next time they find themselves getting angry.

Grade Level

3rd

Materials

- The 14 "Self –Talk Statements For Anger Control" strategies found on the following page written on index cards
- Masking tape
- Additional index cards, one for each student

Time Needed

30 minutes

Objectives

- Students will learn the hand sign for anger control.
- Students will be able to identify triggers for a conflict and angry feelings.
- Students will choose three strategies they like to use to solve conflicts and calm down.

Procedures

- Teach the hand sign for anger control, and have a short discussion about the feeling of anger and how it can get us into trouble.
- Introduce the students to the concept of "self-talk." Tell them this is a powerful way to get our brains in gear and think before we do something that could get us into trouble. Hand out the 14 self-talk phrases printed on index cards to 14 different students.

- Have the students come up one at a time, and read their statement. Ask students to listen carefully to each statement, because they are going to choose three they think might help them in the future when they get mad. After each statement is read, have a short discussion with student's input as to how this could be helpful, then tape the statements on the wall or the board spread around the room.
- When all statements have been read and discussed tell the students when you say "Go" they are to go to their first choice of a statement they think would help them. Make sure you tell them that you would like them to think for themselves and not go somewhere just because a friend is going there.
- Repeat the moving around the room two more times so that each student has chosen three places to stand in front of three positive self-talk statements they can use. Encourage comments from the student during this interaction, as to why they think that statement would work for them.
- Give each student an index card and ask them to write their three statements down and keep them in a good place where they can refer to them from time to time to remind them to talk to themselves in these positive and helpful ways.
- Review the hand sign for anger control in closing.

☞ Discussion Questions

- Have you ever said any of these statements to yourself before?
- Can you think of any additional statements you could say when you are angry to help yourself calm down?
- What is the hardest part about controlling yourself when you are angry?

☞ Variations

- Have some additional cards available so that the students can write down their own ideas for helpful self-talk statements.
- Put the statements in a visible place in the classroom and encourage students to read them when they are angry.

✏ Lesson 33: I'm Talking to Me!

 **Activity**

Directions: Copy and paste each statement on an index card.

SELF-TALK STATEMENTS FOR ANGER CONTROL

I am tired of being in trouble. I am going to think before I do something that will get me in trouble again.

I can stand up for myself. I do not have to hit, run away, or call names just because someone is teasing me. I can use humor, ignore, walk away, or tell my friend they are hurting my feelings.

I can tell my body is getting tight and I am getting angry. I need to take some deep breaths and count to 10. I can do this.

I know when I am getting angry and I can learn to calm down before I say something or do something.

Everyone has angry feelings, and I can too. I can stand up for myself without hurting others. I can stay in control of myself.

It's OK to be angry, but it is not OK to hurt someone else by hitting or saying something mean to them.

I am a strong person. Since I am strong I need to be in control of my actions and words.

ANGER MANAGEMENT

✎ Lesson 33: I'm Talking to Me!

Even though other people do and say things that make me angry I am responsible for what I do about it. I can decide that I want to act calm and in control.

I like the feeling I have when I stand up for myself without getting angry and doing something I shouldn't. It makes me proud to be me.

When I feel like I want to hit, push, or scream at someone I don't have to do it. I can stop, think, and act in a way that does not hurt the other person.

Even though I make mistakes and lose my temper, I do not always have to act this way. I am smart and I can change and do better the next time.

When I don't get my way I can take three deep breaths and remember that it really doesn't matter. Other people want to get their way sometimes too.

I have stayed calm and in control before and I can do it this time too. I believe in myself.

Sometimes when I am angry I am also scared, worried, or embarrassed. I know it is OK to have all these feelings, and it is normal to be confused sometimes. I can be honest with myself and others.

109

© YouthLight Inc.

Lesson 34: Let's Go Fishing

 Overview

Almost all children are the recipients of occasional teasing from their classmates. This lesson is designed to help children handle this teasing without losing their tempers and reacting in negative ways.

 Grade Level

4th

 Materials

- Fishing pole with line but no hook on it
- Construction paper worms made from pattern on following page
- *Simon's Hook* by Karen Burnett
- Paper fish with 5 strategies from book written on it for each student
- Bag of Goldfish crackers

 Time Needed

30 minutes

🖝 **Objectives**

- Students will learn the hand sign for anger control.
- Students will recognize "hooks" people use to try to bait us.
- Students will learn five strategies to use to remain a "free fish."

🖝 **Procedures**

- As you enter the classroom, prop the fishing rod beside the board to engage students' attention. Tell them we will have our fishing lesson in a minute.
- Teach students the hand sign for anger control.
- Lead discussion as to what causes them to lose their tempers. Ask, "Does name calling ever cause you to lose your temper?"
- Read *Simon's Hook*, asking students to pay special attention to the pictures and the names Simon's friends call him. They will love the different pictures, finding Simon and his grandmother in each of the pictures under the sea,

reading the different hooks people send and how the free fish handle them. Also, make sure they notice that the children fishing are the same friends Simon ran from on the playground.

- As you read, list each of Simon's new anger control strategies on the board.
- When book is finished process with the following questions:
  - What was the first hook Simon's friends gave him?
  - How did he react?
  - Did this help him or hurt him? Why?
  - Why do you think people try to bait us?
  - Can we stop other people from sending hooks our way?
  - Who can we control? Remind them of this lesson's hand sign.
  - When Simon returned to the playground at the end of the book, which free fish strategy did he use? Did it work?
  - Look at the difference in his face when he used humor to handle the hook and when he just ran away angry at the beginning of the story.
  - Do we have to bite when someone throws us a hook?
  - Do you think we will get more or less hooks thrown at us if we bite? Why?
- Give out the paper worms and ask each student to write a name they have been called on their worm. (This is also a good way to reinforce that all children get called names sometimes.)
- Take up the worms, mix them up, and tape one on the fishing line of the pole you brought in. Throw it out to someone in the class. When the student catches it, he or she reads the insult aloud and responds with one of the five strategies taught in the book.
- Throw out as many hooks as you have time, encouraging the students who catch them to use different strategies from the five they have to choose from. Ask them if they have any others they could use.
- In closing give each student a construction paper fish with the strategies on it to help them remember to use them. You can also give out Goldfish crackers at this time.
- Close lesson with hand sign for anger control.
- As you see the students around school, ask them if anyone has been fishing near them, and if they are remaining a free fish.

☞ Discussion Questions

- Do you think all children get teased at some time?
- Have you ever felt like Simon when you are being teased?
- Which of Simon's new strategies do you like the best and think you could try the next time someone teases you?

☞ Variations

- As you see the students around the school, ask them if anyone has been fishing near them, and if they are remaining a free fish.
- Help students make construction paper fish that say, "I'm a free fish." Encourage them to wear their fish as a signal that they are learning not to bite.

✎ Lesson 34: Let's Go Fishing

✂ Activity

Directions: Copy and cut out to give to each student.

FREE FISH STRATEGIES

ARE YOU A FREE FISH?
Instead of biting...

1. Do little or nothing.
2. Agree with the hook.
3. Distract the fisherman.
4. Laugh or make a joke.
5. Stay away from the hook.

Burnett, Karen. Simon's Hook. GR Publishing, 2000.

✏️ Lesson 34: Let's Go Fishing

✂️ Activity

Directions: Cut out and use as the bait on the hook of your fishing rod.

WORM PATTERNS

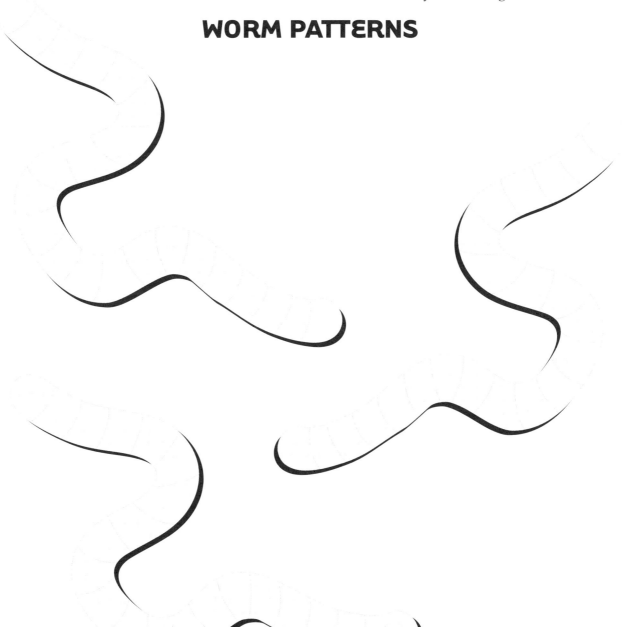

Lesson 35: It's Getting Hot In Here

 ## Overview

This lesson gives students the insight that there are different levels of anger. They also see that conflict is inevitable, and if we learn ways to resolve it early, we do not need to reach the exploding level of anger.

 ## Grade Level

5th

Materials

- Copy and cut apart the "Responses to Conflict" worksheet on p. 116
- Large thermometer on heavy poster paper made from pattern on p. 117

Time Needed

30 minutes

 ## Objectives

- Students will learn the hand sign for anger control.
- Students will recognize degrees of anger.
- Students will understand progression from conflict to anger.
- Students will identify appropriate responses to conflict.

Procedures

- Teach the hand sign for anger control, and talk about how it relates to the sign for self-control or self-discipline. Explain that controlling our anger is another important skill to learn as we become more self-disciplined.
- Arrange three chairs in a small circle in the middle of the room and ask for three volunteers who like to talk. Explain that these students will be the fish in the fishbowl, and the rest of us are going to watch and listen to them without talking.
- Ask the following questions to the three students:
  - What is conflict?
  - What is a fight?

- What is an argument?
- Are all conflicts fights?
- What feeling do we have when we are involved in a conflict or a fight?
- Bring up three different students and ask:
  - What causes conflict?
  - What makes it worse?
  - What cools it off?
  - Name some different groups that have conflict. (families, friends, countries, students and teachers, etc.) Name some specific examples of conflicts these groups may have. As they name them, write them on the board.
  - What may happen when these groups have conflict and lose their tempers? (hurt feelings, a break-up of a marriage or friendship, bad grades, wars, etc.)
- Ask the total class: Are we going to have conflicts? Are we going to get angry?
- Since the answers are yes, then we need to learn to control our anger so that we can figure out how to solve our problem and get along with each other.
- Bring out large thermometer and explain the degrees of anger. Point out that when a conflict first starts we may be on the irritated degree of mad but as it escalates, our anger gets more intense. At a certain level, which is different for all of us, we lose control. So let's talk about what we can do before we get to that level.
- Distribute the "Responses to Conflict" construction paper thermometers. Ask each student to read his or her response and decide where on the anger thermometer scale he or she would be to respond in this way.
- Read examples of conflicts students have suggested, and ask them to tell you some appropriate ways to handle them.
- End the lesson with a review of the anger control hand sign.

☞ Discussion Questions

- How did this lesson help you understand the emotion of anger differently?
- Does understanding anger help you manage it? How?
- Have you ever had a conflict with someone you cared about and felt bad about it later? How did you handle that?

☞ Variations

- Minimize size of anger thermometer, copy and cut out, and give each student one to keep.
- Instead of putting three students in a group to discuss while the class listens, divide class into small groups and give each small group the questions above to discuss.
- Ask students to keep an "anger journal" writing down times and events that make them angry. Offer to talk with them privately about their journal entries and how they handled the conflicts.

✎ Lesson 35: It's Getting Hot In Here

 ✂ Activity Directions: Copy and cut out to give to each student.

RESPONSES TO CONFLICT

- Threaten the other person
- Give in to the other person
- Compromise
- Avoid the other person
- Pretend to agree, then do what you want.
- Change the subject
- Try to forget or ignore the situation
- Whine and complain
- Admit you are wrong
- See it from the other person's point of view
- Call the other person a name
- Talk about it
- Listen to the other person
- Get a friend to be mean to the other person
- Ask for help from an adult
- Say you are sorry
- Ask the other person to apologize
- Walk away
- Take deep breaths
- Count to 20 and think a minute

✎ Lesson 35: It's Getting Hot In Here

 Activity Directions: Copy on card stock and cut out.

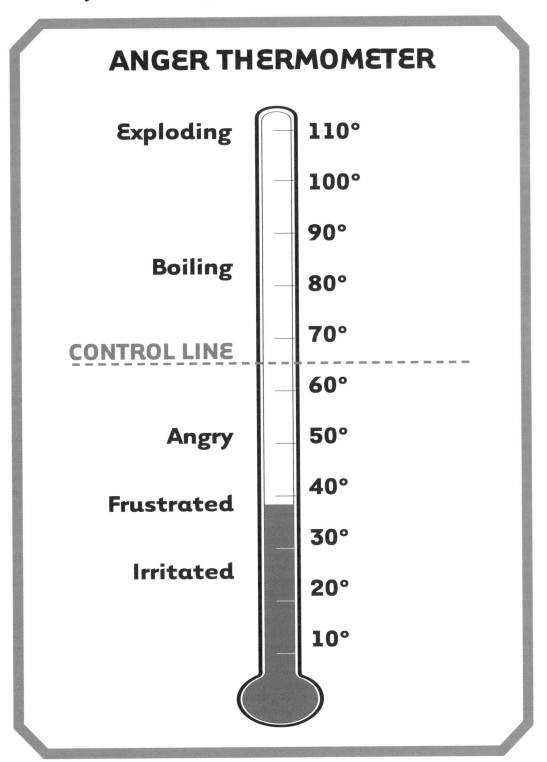

ANGER THERMOMETER

Exploding	110°
	100°
	90°
Boiling	80°
	70°
CONTROL LINE	
	60°
Angry	50°
	40°
Frustrated	30°
Irritated	20°
	10°

COUNSELOR'S CORNER

Dear Parents,

Our lesson and hand sign for today's guidance lesson in your child's classroom was anger control. Anger is an emotion which can confuse and scare children, and part of our lesson focuses on helping them see that it is a healthy, normal emotion. The difficulty, as we adults understand, comes in controlling this powerful emotion so that it does not get us into trouble and/or cause damage to ourselves and others.

In your child's lesson we explored this truth in various ways, and came up with positive strategies to handle our anger. Ask your child what we talked about, and be ready to hear any new ideas he or she learned about anger. Share your own experiences with anger and how you deal with it to help you feel better and more in control. When children hear that adults also struggle with powerful emotions they are comforted, knowing they are not unusual and strange but only human. They love hearing how we are not perfect, and that we too have difficult at times controlling our anger.

When you witness your child's anger building, use the hand sign to encourage anger control, and if he or she is successful, reinforce this sign of maturity with a loving hug and comment, "I am so pleased you are learning to control your anger. I know it makes you feel good too."

Sincerely,

Your School Counselor

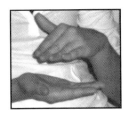

STUDY SKILLS/ SCHOOL ATTITUDE

When students have a positive, "I can" attitude in school they want to learn and therefore achieve success. There are many reasons why a student does not come to the classroom with this attitude, and there are many ways to help him or her improve in this area. Sometimes parents are intimidated or defensive about a child's academic setting, and this is sensed by the child and carried into the classroom. Sometimes a child is all too aware of his or her weaknesses, therefore never noticing the strengths that can be used to help him or her succeed. The following lessons focus on basic skills and attitudes that can help all children learn.

☞ Hand Sign* for this lesson (Pre-K and Kindergarten):

LISTEN   Hold right hand up to right ear with thumb, index finger, and middle finger up, the rest of the fingers curled in. Bend the extended middle and index fingers down two times, like you are bringing sound to the ear.

☞ Hand Signs* for this lesson (1st – 5th grades):

STUDY   Hold left hand open in front of chest, palm facing up. Move the right hand, palm facing down toward the open left hand as you wiggle the fingers of the right hand.

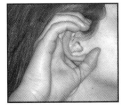

SKILL   Hold the little finger side of the left open hand with the curved right fingers. Pull the right hand forward while closing the fingers of the left hand into the palm.

SCHOOL   Tap the fingers of the right open hand, palm facing down on the left open hand, palm facing up.

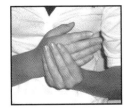

ATTITUDE   Make a fist with right hand, thumb sticking up. Placing hand in front of the heart, make a circular motion with the thumb around the heart, ending with the thumb against the chest.

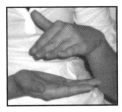

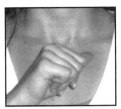

Adapted from Costello, Elaine. Concise American Sign Language Dictionary. Random House. 2000.

Lesson 36: Howdy, Partner

☞ Overview

Young children are used to working with partners. This lesson shows them that two of our body parts, our eyes and our ears, also work together to help us listen better.

☞ Grade Level

Pre-K

☞ Materials

- Copy of big ear and big eye on the following page, backed with poster board

☞ Time Needed

20 minutes

☞ Objectives

- Students will learn the hand sign for listen.
- Students will sing a song about good listening.
- Students will understand the importance of listening to the teacher.

☞ Procedures

- Show students the big ear you have brought. Put it up to your ear and ask them, "Which ear is bigger?" "Which ear do you think can hear better?" "Do our ears have to be big to work well?" "What makes our ears work well?"
- Teach them the hand sign for listen.
- Ask them if they know what a partner is. Demonstrate with a short role play. Have two students come to the front with you and ask them to work together to clean up the blocks you just dropped. Let class watch them work together. Explain that these two students are partners, getting a job done by helping each other.

- Tell them that there is another body part that is a partner to our ears, to help us listen better. Ask them for their ideas as to which body part it might be. After a few answers, show them the big eye you have brought. Tell them our eyes and our ears are partners. When our eyes are looking at who is talking our ears work better! Demonstrate this by giving a few students directions while they are looking at you then have them look away and play with an object while giving the same direction. Most of the time they will not follow the direction as well when they are not looking at you.
- Tell them this is why their teacher asks them to look at her/him when he/she wants them to listen. Let's learn a song today to help us remember this.
- Teach the following song to the tune of *Mary Had a Little Lamb*.

> I have ears that listen well, listen well, listen well.
>   (cup hands around ears as you sing.)
> I have ears that listen well, let me show you how.
>   (point with fingers to audience.)
> Eyes look at the teacher first, teacher first, teacher first
>   (make circles with fingers and put over eyes)
> Eyes look at the teacher first, then my ears work – WOW!

- Review the hand sign for listen and close by reminding students to let their ears and eyes be good partners.

☞ Discussion Questions

- Do adults ever tell you to listen to them? Why do you think they want you to listen?
- What happens sometimes if you do not listen to an adult?
- How does listening help us do better in class?

☞ Variations

- Give out simple questions to students with their eyes closed, then open, and compare how they follow them each time.
- Play a listening game with the children, giving them an instruction one time only. When they can follow one step directions the first time hearing them, then increase the directions to two steps, three, etc. They will enjoy seeing how their listening skills improve when they practice eye contact and good listening skills.

✎ Lesson 36: Howdy, Partner

✂ **Activity** Directions: Copy on card stock, cut out, and take to class.

EAR PATTERN

✏ Lesson 36: Howdy, Partner

✂ **Activity** Directions: Copy on card stock, cut out, and take to class.

EYE PATTERN

Lesson 37: Get That Ear in Gear

 Overview

Children hear the instruction to listen many times during the day. This lesson shows them in a fun game how challenging it is to be a good listener, and lets them practice following instructions after hearing them only one time.

 Grade Level

Kindergarten

 Materials

- Puppet friend

 Time Needed

20 minutes

Objectives

- Students will learn the hand sign for listen.
- Students will learn the importance of listening in class.
- Students will practice listening carefully the first time something is said.

Procedures

- Before teaching this lesson's hand sign, have a conversation with your puppet asking him if he is a good listener. Ask him why it is important to be a good listener, and when he cannot think of reasons ask the class to help you. Emphasize answers such as: "it helps us to know what to do; we don't get fussed at; we are ready when we are supposed to be; the teacher doesn't get as tired helping us," etc.
- Teach the hand sign for listen. Tell students that this is a very important skill they need in order to be good students, and that sometimes we think it is easy to be good listeners but it isn't. It takes practice, just like learning any new skill.

- Tell children that today they are going to play a game to practice being good listeners in class. Send one child out of the room and hide an object like a book or block somewhere in the room. Tell the children that you are going to give the child who is waiting outside directions to find the object, but you will not repeat each direction once you have said it. Their job is to sit quietly, watch the student, and listen to the directions as well.
- Call the child back in the room and give the initial direction such as, "Come to the front of the room near the computer center." Go through the directions one at a time until the item is found. Ask the children who thinks he or she could do it next, if it gets a little harder. Send another volunteer out of the room.
- This time, when the child returns, give directions two at a time, again only saying them once. Encourage the child to look at you as you talk, to focus on what you say, and not to talk to anyone else as he listens. When he has found the item tell the class that this is just the way they should be listening to their teacher when he/she talks to them. They should always practice looking at him/her, focusing on what he/she is saying, and not talking to others because that makes it hard to remember what they are hearing.
- As time allows, let other students have a turn. Save time at the end of the lesson to give multiple directions to the whole class such as, "stand on your right foot, hop three times, and put your hands on your head." Do a few of these strings of instructions to help them practice watching you as you speak, listening the first time, and concentrating on what you say.
- In closing, review the hand sign for listen, and tell children to keep practicing their good listening skills.

☞ Discussion Questions

- Which is easier, listening in school or listening at home? Why do you think so?
- How does it make you feel when someone really listens to you?
- Can you think of a time when being a good listener resulted in something special happening?

☞ Variations

- Ask class what are some of the directions their teacher gives them. Practice these in a string of more than one at a time also.
- Encourage students to play the listening game with each other during the next rainy day recess.

Lesson 38: Stop, Look, and Listen

 **Overview**

Using friendly competition, this lesson lets students experience the challenge of establishing good school habits. The lesson focuses on learning to use their eyes and ears well by concentrating as they listen and learn.

Grade Level

1st

Materials

- Puppet
- Small objects to spread out on table in classroom, i.e. colored markers, tape, small toys and/or cars, books, child's hat or glove, etc.
- Listening Challenges worksheet on the following page

Time Needed

30 minutes

Objectives

- Students will learn the hand signs for listen, school, and attitude.
- Students will practice remembering what they see and hear.
- Students will understand the importance of using eyes and ears in school.

Procedures

- Have a conversation with your puppet with the puppet telling you how she is not doing well in school. When you ask her why she tells you that her teacher says she is not using her eyes and ears in class. Ask puppet if she would like the class to help her solve this problem. When she says yes, ask class, "What do you think the teacher means by this?" Elicit responses then tell children that today we will play a game to help us practice using our eyes and ears better and maybe this will help our puppet friend too.
- Teach the hand signs for listen, school, and attitude. Make sure children know what attitude means and why it is important in school. Role play with puppet a student who comes to class with an attitude that shows she wants to learn

and one who comes with a disruptive, noncaring attitude. Ask, "Which student will learn more today?" Encourage children to talk to someone if they are grumpy so they can get the mad out and be ready to learn.

- Divide class into four teams and tell students we are going to play the Stop, Look and Listen game. We will see which team is using their ears and eyes the best today. Ask the first team to put their heads down and arrange a table in front of the room with 6 objects. Ask the team to open their eyes, come to the front of the room, look carefully at the objects, then return to their seats and put their heads down. When they have returned to their seats, take away two of the objects. Have them return to the front and tell you what two objects are missing. As the rest of class is watching, tell them the importance of concentrating on what we see when the teacher is teaching us so that our brains can remember to use the information later. Allow each team to do this, giving points for the number of objects they remember.

- Tell students the next task is to concentrate with their ears listening and see if they can do just what I say the first time. Sometimes we get used to having instructions repeated and it is so much better to listen the first time so that we are ready immediately. Using the Listening Challenges worksheet, call out directions to each team in turn. Give points for the number of directions they do correctly without you repeating them. Encourage them to help each other on their team.

- Reward winning team with a standing ovation from class. Bring puppet back out, and ask her what she learned today. She says, "I learned not to come to class angry and grumpy. I can talk to my teacher or counselor to help me feel better so I can do my best work. I also learned to look and listen carefully as the teacher is talking so that my brain will work better and help me remember what he/she says. Thank you, class, for helping me with this problem."

- Close lesson with review of the three hand signs.

☞ Discussion Questions

- Which game was harder for you to do well in – using your eyes well or using your ears well?
- What are some good things that have happened to you when you were being a good listener?
- Have you ever come to school grumpy in the morning? Did this make it harder for you to pay attention and do well in your work?

☞ Variations

- Set up a quiet corner in the room where students can go if they come to school in a bad mood. Encourage them to draw, write, or talk about what is bothering them so that they can feel better and have a good attitude about their day.
- Point out positive, helpful attitudes as you see them in the class, in a story you are reading to the students, or in a co-worker so that they will increase their understanding of the importance of attitude in life.

Lesson 38: Stop, Look, and Listen

 Activity

Directions: These directions are given to each team in turn. Each set has four basic commands. Give each team 1 point for each command they do correctly.

LISTENING CHALLENGES

TEAM ONE:

(1). Line up with tallest student at the end of line, shortest at front
(2).Walk in a line to the class door
(3). Each student tap on door four times
 (4). Return to me

TEAM TWO:

(1). Sit in a circle in the reading center
(2). All students raise your right hand
(3). Say your name out loud
(4). Clap two times

Lesson 38: Stop, Look, and Listen

TEAM THREE:

(1). Stand together near the window in a line

(2) Look out the window

(3). Say together, "What a beautiful day"

(4). Turn around to face the class and smile

TEAM FOUR:

(1). Line up at front of room facing the class

(2). Open your mouths wide and say "ahhh"

(3). Jump up and down three times counting as you jump

(4). Say, "Yea, we did it"

Lesson 39: Map to Success

☞ Overview

Using a game format this lesson helps students see that succeeding in school is a process, and there are challenges along the way. The game guides them to identify the major obstacles in the way of success and how they can overcome them.

☞ Grade Level

2nd

☞ Materials

- Road Map
- Copies of "School Success Map" found on the following page for each student
- "Challenges to School Success" cards found on p. 133, copied and cut apart

☞ Time Needed

30 minutes

☞ Objectives

- Students will learn the hand signs for study, skill, school, and attitude.
- Students will identify three sources of help with school challenges.
- Students will understand how to help themselves succeed.

☞ Procedures

- Teach students the four hand signs for lesson: study, skill, school, and attitude. Discuss why they think the sign for attitude is made in front of the heart. Ask them, "What is attitude? Why is it important in all we do? Have any of you ever heard a coach talk about attitude on the team?" Make sure all students know this word and why it is important.
- Bring out road map and ask, "What is this?" "How does it help us?" (In the days of GPS systems, some may have to be reminded what this is!) Ask why we sometimes need help in finding our way. Answers can include: we don't know everything; we forget our way sometimes, we get lost or confused, we

are going somewhere we have never been, etc. Put these answers on the board, then tell children, "Today we are going to learn that for us to succeed in school we need a map also."

- Looking at what is written on board compare the need for a map in school to needing a map on a trip. Remind them of why we need road maps. "We certainly don't know everything, we sometimes forget what we learned before, we get confused and feel lost, and we are learning new things we have never seen before. Just like we can't get to our destination on the road without help from a map, we can't succeed in school without this help either."

- Distribute the "School Success Maps." Tell students you are going to read some "Challenges to School Success" cards that show some problems a student might have. They are to decide what would be helpful if they had this problem - their Mind, their Attitude, or People. Then they are to write either a M for Mind, an A for Attitude, or a P for People on the path. Sometimes they may write more than one letter per block. Point out these letters and their meaning from the legend at the bottom of the map.

- Read the "Challenges to School Success" cards one at a time and have children move one space at a time along the map toward Success, writing one or more of the letters on the spaces on their maps that would help them with the problem you read. Do this until they have found their way to Success at the end of their maps. During the "journey," after you have read out some of your situations, encourage the students to volunteer some of the problems they have that may get in their way of succeeding in school. Let them decide which letter, M/A/ or P, could go in the space. As you are reading the challenges the children will see themselves, and realize how they can help themselves with each of these problems by using their Mind, their Attitude, or the People who want to help them.

- Encourage students to remember these three words, Mind/Attitude/ and People, as they continue working to succeed in school. Close with review of today's hand signs.

☞ Discussion Questions

- Can you think of some other things that would be helpful if you are having problems in school besides your mind, your attitude, or other people?
- Who are some specific people who can help you?
- In what ways does a good attitude help us be successful in school?

☞ Variations

- Have the children write a journal entry about a school problem they have had and how they resolved it. With permission from the writer, share these with the class.
- Put a copy of the "School Success Map" on the class bulletin board and let the students write in their problems and how they solved them.

✎ Lesson 39: Map to Success

✂ Activity

Directions: Put an M, an A, or a P (or a combination of the three letters) on each numbered line as you hear the 20 challenges to school success read aloud.

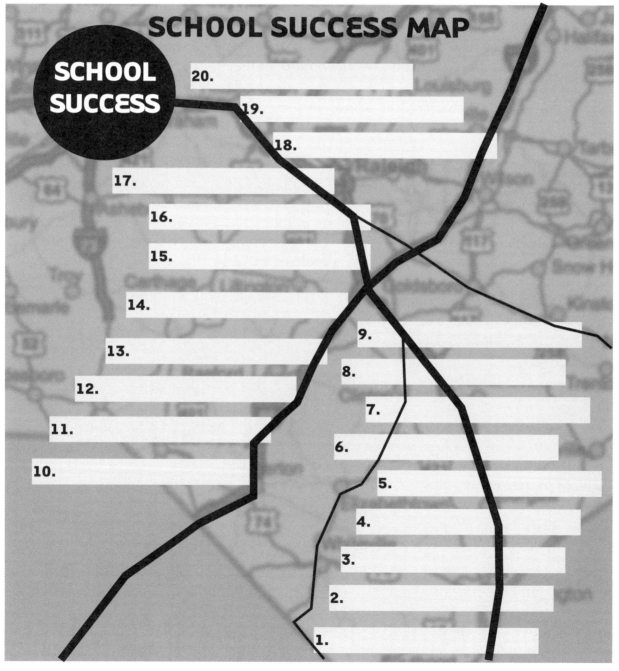

SCHOOL SUCCESS MAP

SCHOOL SUCCESS

20.
19.
18.
17.
16.
15.
14.
13.
12.
11.
10.
9.
8.
7.
6.
5.
4.
3.
2.
1.

M = Mind   A = Attitude   P = People to help me

✎ Lesson 39: Map to Success

 **Activity**

Directions: Copy these onto card stock and cut out.

CHALLENGES TO SCHOOL SUCCESS CARDS

You get up late and are feeling grumpy and rushed when you get to school.	**You know you are better in math than in reading.**
You forget your signed papers.	**Your teacher seems mad at you and you don't know why.**
You can't remember the way to do the math problem.	**You go to bed late and are very tired today.**
You think your friend likes someone better than you.	**You like to read, but don't like math.**
You have a test tomorrow.	**You need to finish a book by tomorrow.**
You want to read harder books like your friend.	**You have to learn a certain number of math facts by next week.**
Someone laughed when you asked a question.	**You are worried about the big test tomorrow.**
You don't understand the science lesson at all.	**You don't think you can do the assignment, because you are confused.**
You got in trouble for talking while the teacher was explaining the work.	**You want to play outside, but you are not through your homework.**
Your friend asks you to help her with the math.	**You forgot to study your spelling words last night.**

Lesson 40: It's A Hit!

 Overview

Using the format of the game of baseball this lesson helps students identify both helpful and non-helpful behaviors for school success. They will enjoy the friendly competition while recognizing the importance of a good attitude and good study habits.

 Grade Level

3rd

 Materials

- "School Behavior Baseballs" worksheet copied and cut apart

 Time Needed

30 minutes

 Objectives

- Students will learn the hand signs for study, skill, school, and attitude.
- Students will identify helpful and non-helpful behaviors and attitudes in school.
- Students will add to counselor's list of attitudes and behaviors.

 Procedures

- Teach hand signs for study, skill, school, and attitude. Have a short discussion on these four words, including asking students why they think hand signs are done the way they are. Elicit comments such as: study looks like reading, school looks like teacher clapping for attention, and the sign for attitude sign is made near the heart.
- Divide class into two teams. Let them name themselves if they wish. Tell them we will be playing a baseball game, and you will be pitching. The balls you will pitch are behaviors and attitudes that help or hurt your school progress. If

you get a ball that causes a problem it is an out, if you get a ball that will help you, you get on base. The team with the most runs at the end of the game is the winner.

- Start the game using the "School Behavior Baseballs." About halfway through the game, give out the blank balls and ask students to write their own idea of a behavior or attitude that could help or hurt their progress in school. Incorporate these, as appropriate, in the last few innings of the game.
- Give the winning team a standing ovation. Remind students how much attitude helps or hurts us, and of the many behaviors we can do by ourselves and with others' help to succeed in school.
- Close lesson with review of the hand signs.

☞ Discussion Questions

- Where have you heard the word "attitude" before today's lesson?
  What does the word mean to you?
- What is the difference between a good attitude and skill?
  Can you develop both? How?
- Can you think of a time when having a good attitude helped you in school or with your friends?

☞ Variations

- At the 7th inning stretch, allow students to stretch and eat popcorn.
- Collect news stories about movie stars, sports heroes, politicians, etc. who have shown a good attitude, and share these stories with the students. Encourage them to look for these kinds of stories to help them maintain a good attitude when they are getting discouraged.

Lesson 40: It's A Hit!

 **Activity**

Directions: Copy, cut out, and use in the game.

SCHOOL BEHAVIOR BASEBALLS

You have all your school supplies when you come to school every morning.

You left your homework on the kitchen table.

You lost your papers that were supposed to be signed.

You studied while watching TV last night.

You went to bed early because you knew you had a test today.

You were talking while the teacher explained the assignment.

You enjoy looking out the window a lot during class.

You had a ball game and did not get your homework done.

You asked your mother to call out your spelling words for a quick review on the way to school.

You got angry when your teacher made you do your paper over again.

You hurried through your test so you could go to the reading center first.

You took your time on your test, and were one of the last ones through.

You asked your mother to call out your spelling words for a quick review on the way to school.

You got angry when your teacher made you do your paper over again.

You hurried through your test so you could go to the reading center first.

You took your time on your test, and were one of the last ones through.

136

✏ Lesson 40: It's A Hit!

You let someone else copy your homework.

You told a friend you would help her with her math facts, but she could not copy your homework.

You asked your teacher to help you.

You asked a question.

You laughed at someone who asked a question.

You volunteered to read to the younger students during a school project.

You told your teacher the truth about why you did not have your homework.

You told your mom you felt bad when you didn't so you wouldn't have to go to school on a test day.

You did not ask for help when you couldn't understand something.

You practiced your math facts while riding in the car on a trip with your family.

You talk to your parents about what you are doing in class every day.

You invite your parents to come to school for PTA meetings and other programs.

You smile at your teacher and classmates.

You encourage others when they are having a hard time.

You don't get up when you are called in the morning so you are late for school.

You get up in the morning so you are not late to school.

You wait until the last minute to start on the science project.

You are worried about school because you did not read the assignment.

Lesson 41: Touchdown!

 Overview

This lesson compares success on the gridiron with success in the classroom. While playing a fun game, students look at the different sets of rules, penalties, skills needed, rewards earned, and the role of coaches, referees, and teammates in both football and school.

 Grade Level

4th

 Materials

- Sport trophy
- Six copies of "Football Vs. School" worksheet on page 140
- Copy of "Goals" worksheet on page 141 for each student

 Time Needed

30 minutes

 Objectives

- Students will learn hand signs for study, skill, school, and attitude.
- Students will work cooperatively to understand ways school is like a game.
- Students will identify rules, penalties, and rewards for playing the school game well.

 **Procedures**

- Tell students that today we are going to learn sign language for four very important words that will help them be happy and successful every day. Give them a few minutes to guess what these words might be, then show them the signs for study, skill, school, and attitude without telling them the words you are signing. After a few have guessed, tell them the four words and let them practice signing them as well. Continue the discussion asking them why these are important.

- Bring out the sport trophy, and ask students to relate the importance of attitude to success in school to importance of attitude in success on the ball field. Tell them that there are many similarities between the games we play and coming to school. We are going to explore these similarities together today.
- Divide students into teams of 4-6. Give each team a copy of "Football Vs School" worksheet, asking them to complete the page as a group.
- After 15 minutes of working together, regroup the total class and have them report their answers. Encourage them to share any discussion, disagreements, or interesting questions that came up as they worked together.
- Review hand signs and encourage students to ask their various coaches, teammates, and referees when they need help in winning the game of school.

☞ Discussion Questions

- In what ways do you see school and sports being alike? In what ways are they different?
- How can having a good attitude help you in sports and school alike?
- How do you feel when you lose in a sports event? Is this feeling similar to having a problem in school and not doing well on a certain test or project?
- How do you feel when you win a sports event? Is this feeling similar to getting a good grade and knowing you have done your best on a test or project?

☞ Variations

- Give students a homework assignment to interview a coach or referee, asking him/her how attitude is important in the game.
- Invite a high school coach to talk to the class about the importance of attitude, practice, and school in being successful in whatever we do.

✎ Lesson 41: Touchdown!

Directions: Complete the worksheet with your team.

FOOTBALL VS. SCHOOL — TWO GAMES IN LIFE

	SCHOOL	FOOTBALL
Four Important Rules	1. _____ 2. _____ 3. _____ 4. _____	1. _____ 2. _____ 3. _____ 4. _____
Penalties if Rules Disobeyed		
Skills Needed To Succeed		
Rewards if You Play Well		
Role of Coach, Referee, and Teammates		

✎ Lesson 41: Touchdown!

Directions: List four goals you want to accomplish in school.

1. _____

2. _____

3. _____

4. _____

Lesson 42: We're Stylin'

 **Overview**

Students are encouraged to try their best in school when they realize that everyone has his or her own learning style. Recognizing their own personal strengths gives them more confidence and pride in their work, attitudes essential for success in school.

Grade Level

5th

Materials

- Pictures from magazines or catalogs of men and women dressed in different types of clothes and with different hairstyles
- A cookie cutter
- Index cards
- Copy of "What's My Style" for each student

Time Needed

30 minutes

Objectives

- Students will learn hand signs for study, skill, school, and attitude.
- Students will learn synonyms for skill.
- Students will identify their individual styles of learning.

Procedures

- Teach students the hand signs for study, skill, school, and attitude. Have a short discussion on these words, asking students why they are important. List on the board the following synonyms of "skill:" ability, able, capable, efficient, expert, handy, proficient, talent. Ask them if everyone is talented and skillful in everything.

- Explain that learning is like this. We all have ways we are skillful in learning, and one of our jobs is to discover what way we learn the best to help ourselves keep a good attitude in school.
- Hold up the cookie cutter, and ask students how this is used. Elaborate that when making cookies, each looks just alike because of the cookie cutter. To show the opposite, bring out pictures of the men and women you brought. Ask, "Are these cookie cutter people? Do they all look alike?" Let students notice the different styles of clothes, hair, make-up, etc. Explain that our brains are like this, they work differently just like these individuals wear different clothes and hair styles. None are bad or good, they just are. We do not have cookie cutter brains. Our lesson today will help you discover how you learn and how you can be a better student knowing something about your learning style.
- Share Gardner's multiple intelligences concept explaining his seven styles of intelligence using the detailed information on the following page.
- Distribute the "What's My Style" worksheets found on p.145, and ask students to put a check mark beside the two styles that sound most like them. To help them in this task you can repeat the information about the seven styles as they work.
- Group students in small groups of 2-3, and ask them to share which type of intelligence they have with each other. Ask the classmates to help each other determine this.
- Regroup the total class, and review the hand signs of the lesson.

☞ Discussion Questions

- What surprised you about what you learned today on learning styles?
- How can you use your particular style to do your best in the classroom?
- What did you learn about someone in your small group that you did not know?
- Were the students in your small group helpful as you determined your learning style?

☞ Variations

- Give the students a homework assignment to take the learning style sheet home and compare the results they got on themselves with what their parents' style is. Have a class discussion on the findings.
- Help students make a graph of the different learning styles in the room and the grade. Celebrate the different ways of learning with cookies of different shapes and colors.

✎ Lesson 42: We're Stylin'

SEVEN STYLES OF INTELLIGENCE*

1. VISUAL SPATIAL INTELLIGENCE	You are good at puzzles, understanding charts and graphs, and have a good sense of direction. You think in pictures, more than words. You have a good imagination and like to daydream. You can fix and build things with tools, and may have even designed something on your own. When the teacher assigns a project that includes building a model you are ready to go! You would also do well on an assignment that involves drawing or working with pictures.
2. VERBAL LINGUISTIC INTELLIGENCE	You are good with words. You can speak easily and well, and have no problem communicating with others. You think in words, not pictures. You can write stories easily, explain information to others, and understand the meaning of words others are using when they speak to you. You can convince someone else your point of view by talking about it. You learn best by reading, speaking, writing, or discussing.
3. LOGICAL MATHEMATICAL INTELLIGENCE	You are good with numbers, and using reason and logic. You are curious about the world around you, ask lots of questions, and like to do experiments. You can make connections between pieces of information well. You like to solve problems, and you understand patterns. You learn well doing experiments and working with patterns, relationships, and categories.
4. BODILY KINESTHETIC INTELLIGENCE	You are great at movement or dance. You handle objects skillfully, have a good sense of balance and eye-hand coordination, and do well in sports. You enjoy hands on experiments, crafts, acting, and using tools. You learn best when you can move around and touch the material.
5. MUSICAL RHYTHMIC INTELLIGENCE	You love to listen to and produce music, whether it is through an instrument or your own voice. You think in sounds and patterns. You may be very sensitive to sounds around the room and outside such as birds, bells, scraping of chairs in the classroom, etc. You can sing, whistle, remember the tune of songs, and clap out a rhythm easily. You learn best by putting the information to music or rhythm.
6. INTERPERSONAL INTELLIGENCE	You have the ability to relate to and understand others' point of view. You are interested in understanding how others feel and think. You can organize and lead others, and like to keep peace in the group. Sometimes you are called on to resolve conflicts others are having. You like to cooperate when you can, and expect others to do the same. You are also a good listener, and can communicate with others verbally and non-verbally. You learn best by sharing information, working in small groups and comparing views and understandings of others to your own.
7. INTRAPERSONAL INTELLIGENCE	You are interested in knowing all about yourself, and try to understand all your feelings, dreams, strengths, and weaknesses. Because of this, you know yourself better than most of your peers and you are constantly reasoning with yourself and setting goals. You like to work alone and think about things privately. You learn best doing self-paced projects, having personal space, and alone time to think about what you are doing and need to do.

*Gardner, Howard. Frames of Mind, The Theory of Multiple Intelligences. Basic Books. 1993.

✎ Lesson 42: We're Stylin'

Directions: Read the seven styles of learning. Put a check mark in the squares beside the two styles most like you.

WHAT'S MY STYLE?*

1. **Visual/Spatial Intelligence**
   (Good at puzzles, charts, tools, good sense of direction, like to draw)

2. **Verbal/Linguistic Intelligence**
   (Good with words, spelling, speaking, writing, and discussing)

3. **Logical/Mathematical Intelligence**
   (Good with numbers, logic, and like experiments and solving problems)

4. **Bodily/Kinesthetic Intelligence**
   (Good at movement, sports, and dance and enjoy hands on experiments)

5. **Musical/Rhythmic Intelligence**
   (Good at music, singing, rhythms, and very sensitive to all sounds)

6. **Interpersonal Intelligence**
   (Good at understanding other points of view, organizing and leading, listening to others, and working in groups)

7. **Intrapersonal Intelligence**
   (Good at understanding yourself, setting goals, doing independent work, enjoy your privacy and alone time)

Gardner, Howard. Frames of Mind, The Theory of Multiple Intelligences. Basic Books. 1993.

Dear Parents,

Today's classroom guidance lesson was on study skills and school attitude. The younger students learned the hand sign for listen. The older students learned the signs for study, skill, school, and attitude. These signs symbolize important truths in what makes a successful student.

Since listening skills are so crucial our lesson emphasized the important and sometimes difficult task of hearing and responding to what is asked the first time. Sometimes children are so used to having directions repeated that they get in the habit of not paying attention until we raise our voices and say it repeatedly. One way you can help with this at home is to help them get out of this habit, say a direction once and expect them to follow it. Of course this means we must get their attention first so they also need to learn to look at an adult when spoken to.

Attitude is such an important part of everyone's success in life. We all know stories of people who had many things against them, but because of a positive attitude did amazing things in life. As you hear of these stories, see them on TV, etc. use them as teaching moments to help your child see how important attitude is to all of us, young and old.

Below are listed some additional ways you can model and support a healthy attitude towards school for you child:

- Look at your child as an individual with strengths and weaknesses, and help him or her develop the strengths and work on improving the weaknesses, keeping in mind that they may not excel at everything and that is OK.
- Ask for help if you sense a particular problem developing. The teacher's perspective is always helpful in understanding what is expected.
- Remember that we, school and parents, are in this together for the success of your child. Support your child's teachers and school by attending conferences and programs, making sure that homework is done, etc.
- Help your child have access to hobbies, activities, and other avenues to develop his or her interests and strengths.
- Model reading and learning at home.
- Encourage continuing to try as he or she experiences learning struggles. Celebrate progress, however small, in difficult areas.
- Help your child look ahead to how education will help in his or her future.

Sincerely,

Your School Counselor

CAREER AWARENESS

Young children have dreams of what they want to be "when they grow up." What an opportunity it is for us to take these dreams and encourage, nurture, and expand them as our students grow. Finding meaningful, challenging, and productive work as a young adult can be exciting, or confusing and terrifying, depending on how well the individual is prepared for the career world. During the elementary years, our job as counselors is to help our students develop an awareness of the world outside school, to realize the abundant and ever changing job market, and to learn how to fit their particular skills and interests into that world. These lessons on careers are designed to match the appropriate developmental level of the students. Have fun with them!

☞ Hand Sign* for this lesson:

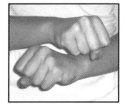

WORK   Make fists with both hands. Tap the heel of the right hand, palm facing forward, two times on the back of the left fist which is held in front of the body, palm facing down.

Adapted from Costello, Elaine. Concise American Sign Language Dictionary. Random House. 2000.

Lesson 43: 1-2-3, What Will I Be?

☞ Overview

Young children love to think about what they want to be when they grow up. This lesson allows them to do that while at the same time planting the seeds that there are many options to explore as they continue to grow and change.

☞ Grade Level

Pre-K

☞ Materials

- Copy and cut apart the career pictures on the following page.
- Puppet friend

☞ Time Needed

20 minutes

☞ Objectives

- Students will learn the hand sign for work.
- Students will role play and identify different types of jobs.
- Students will choose one or two jobs that interest them.

☞ Procedures

- Start the lesson with a conversation with your puppet. She is confused about what she wants to be when she grows up. Tell her she has lots of time to decide, but maybe while you are here in the class the children can give her some ideas. She is very excited about this, so you ask the children if they would like to help. When they say "yes" tell them we will play a game together to learn about jobs and work.
- Teach the hand sign for work. Tell the children that when they grow up there will be lots of things they can do, and that right now their work is school. Everything they learn in the classroom will help them be good workers in the community some day.

- Bring out the set of pictures of people doing different jobs. Using volunteers, have one child at a time come up and look at the picture without anyone else seeing it. Ask the student to act out that job. You may have to help some children with this, but many will be able to do it quite well by themselves. When the class guesses the job, put the picture up so all can see, then go to the next one.
- After all the jobs have been acted out, ask the puppet if any of them look interesting to her. Have her say something like, " Well, I draw well, and I like teaching my little brother so maybe I could be an art teacher some day." Tell the puppet that she is doing some great thinking because if we get a job doing what we like and what we are good at we will do it well.
- Ask the children to take a long look at the pictures and choose one they think is interesting. Call out each job one at a time and ask the children to stand if they would like to do that someday. Let them stand more than once of course, and process this as you go along, helping them to see that different students stand at different times. Remind them that we will each choose what we want to do someday, and it is our decision.
- End the lesson with a review of the hand sign.

☞ Discussion Questions

- What jobs did you see pictures of today that you had not thought of before?
- What is your job right now?
- How can doing a good job in school help you have a good job when you are an adult?

☞ Variations

- Repeat the title of the lesson as a jingle (1-2-3, What Will I Be?) and at the end each child freezes in a stance that looks like a particular job.
- Let children take turns reporting on what their parents do for a career. They could bring pictures of their parents at work for a class bulletin board.

✎ Lesson 43: 1-2-3, What Will I Be?

✂ Activity

Directions: Copy and cut out to use in Lesson 43.

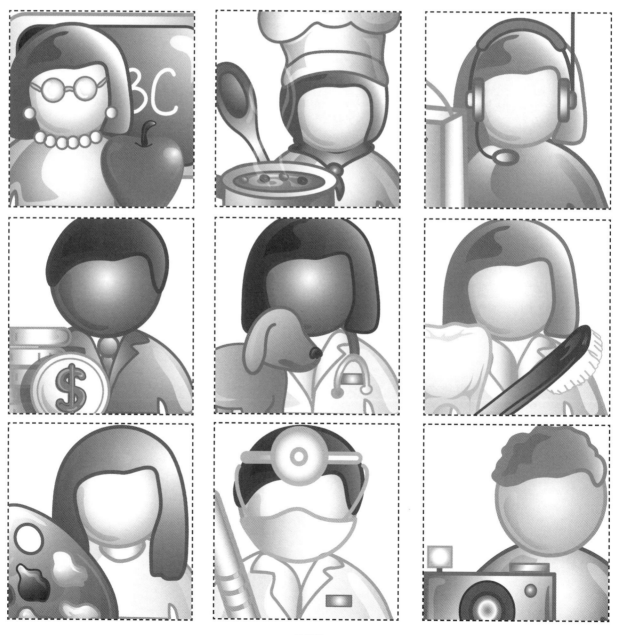

Lesson 43: 1-2-3, What Will I Be?

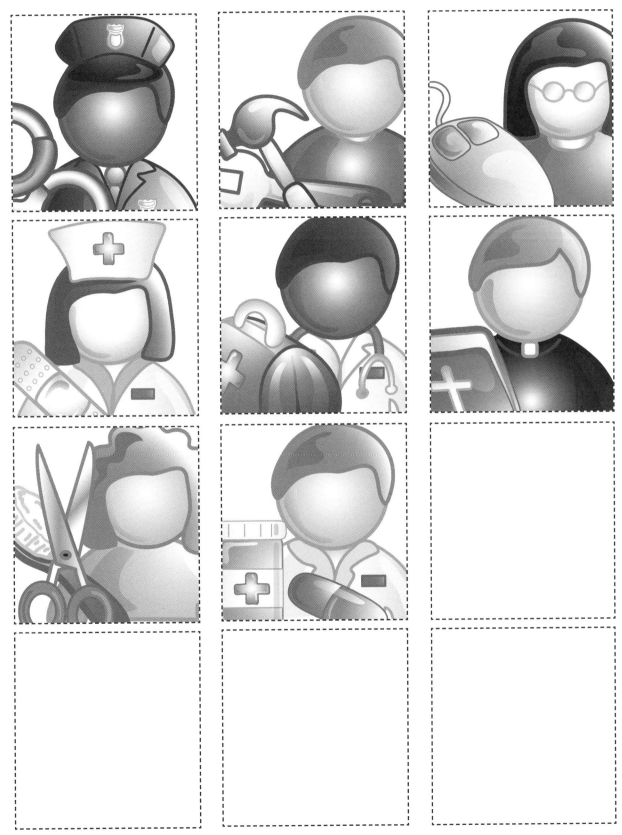

Lesson 44: Tools of the Trade

👉 Overview

This lesson provides the young child a link to various jobs through a variety of tools. As different careers are discussed, the seed is also planted that the children already have a job – school.

👉 Grade Level

Kindergarten

👉 Materials

- A bag of tools and pictures representing different jobs such as: hair dryer, pencil, computer, paint/ markers/ or crayons, hammer, band aids, ace bandages, books, telescope, medicine bottle, baking or cooking utensils, dancing shoes, hoe or rake, baby toys, pad for taking orders in restaurant, microphone, mail bag, etc. (Many of these items can be found in your own home or at the dollar store.)

👉 Time Needed

20 minutes

👉 Objectives

- Students will learn the hand sign for work.
- Students will identify tools that go along with different jobs.
- Students will understand that school is their job right now.

👉 Procedures

- Teach the hand sign for work. Tell students that today's lesson is going to help them see the different jobs that people have, and the tools they use to do them.
- Ask children the meaning of the word "tool." After students share, tell them that many jobs use tools, and that you have a bag with you today with some special tools for different jobs. Explain that they have a long time before they have to decide what they will do for a living some day, but that it is fun to think about it from time to time and see how many choices they will have someday.

- Dig into your bag and bring out each of the tools you brought one at a time. The children will enjoy talking about the tool, telling you the job that goes with that tool, who they may know in that job, and if they have ever used that tool before.
- When the bag is empty, get up and go around the room picking up various items in the kindergarten room and putting them in your bag. As the children watch tell them you are collecting some tools for another very important job.
- Bring out the tools one at a time and ask them what job do you do when you need all these tools: paper, books, pencils, markers, crayons, blocks, numbers, toys from centers, etc. After you have all the tools laid out if no one guesses tell them that these are the tools for being a kindergarten student. Each of them uses these tools every day to do their job, being a student in this class. The better you work and do your job right now, the better you will do in a job as an adult. Keep working and learning and using your tools!
- End lesson with review of the hand sign for work.

☞ Discussion Questions

- Who decides what job you will have some day?
- Which of these tools look interesting to you? Would everyone in the class be interested in the same tools?
- What other tools can you think of that a person would need to do a particular job?

☞ Variations

- Construct a class bulletin board of tools needed to do a good job in school.
- Set up an art table for students to draw a picture of themselves in a career when they grow up.

Lesson 45: Five Up, Five Down

👉 Overview

Children enjoy playing this classroom game as they explore the world of work. They also get to think about what careers interest them at this point, and they gain an awareness of how many options they have.

👉 Grade Level

1st

👉 Materials

- Copy and cut apart the set of 25 careers on the following page.

👉 Time Needed

30 minutes

👉 Objectives

- Students will learn the hand sign for work.
- Students will hear about variety of careers.
- Students will identify one or two that interest them.

👉 Procedures

- Teach students the hand sign for work.
- Tell students that today we are going to play a game to learn about some possible jobs we may like to have some day.
- Hold up the pictures of careers and go through each briefly identifying the job so every child understands what every job is. Since these will be basic jobs, most children will know what they are.
- Put one picture on the corner of each student's desk, telling them that it does not mean that is the job they will have some day, it is just how we are going to play the game. Tell them they will need to remember what card they were given. Use this as a way to address how we do choose our jobs. Does the school counselor, teacher, or parent tell us what we have to do? No, we make our own decision when we are older and ready for such decisions.

154

- After all the pictures have been given out, bring five children to the front of the room. The other children will put their heads down and shut their eyes, and the children at the front will quietly go to a desk and pick up a job they are interested in and return to the front of the room with the picture or card behind their backs.
- When each of the five has finished choosing his or her card, the seated students will pick their heads up and the ones who are missing a card raise their hands. These students will tell the class what career they had on their desk and who they think has it from the five at the front of the room. This allows the class to assess the interests, skills, and personalities of the children at the front of the room and relate those qualities to a particular career.
- This game also acquaints the students to a few career choices they might not have thought of before. As they play, continue to reinforce who makes this decision some day, that they have a long time before they have to decide, and that right now their job is school.
- Close lesson with review of the hand sign for work.

☞ Discussion Questions

- Who chooses what job you will have someday?
- Who are some people who can help you learn more about lots of jobs?
- Were you surprised at the jobs some of your classmates were interested in?

☞ Variations

- Shuffle all the cards, have a student pick one, and act out that job for the students to guess what he/she is doing.
- Pick out a job from the pile and ask the students how doing well in school would be important to this job.

✎ Lesson 45: Five Up, Five Down

✂ Activity

Directions: Copy on card stock, laminate, and cut apart to use in class game.

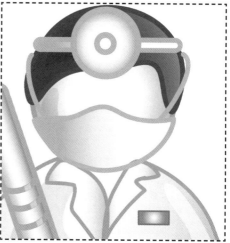

CAREER AWARENESS

✏ Lesson 45: Five Up, Five Down

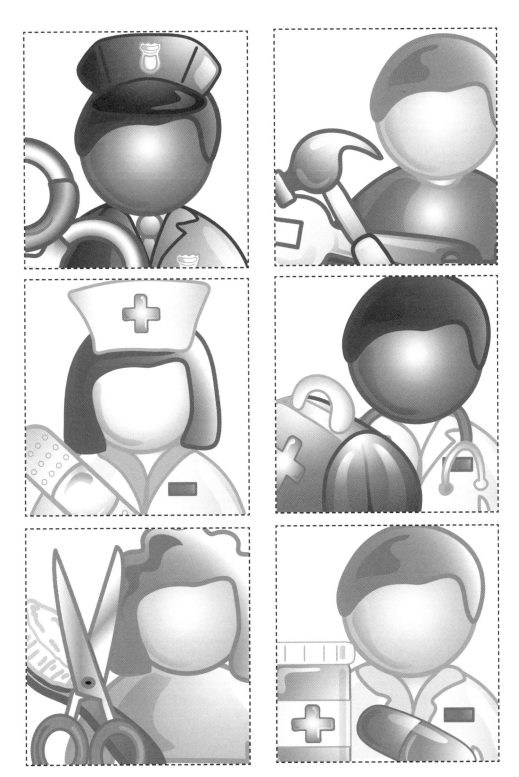

✎ Lesson 45: Five Up, Five Down

✎ Lesson 45: Five Up, Five Down

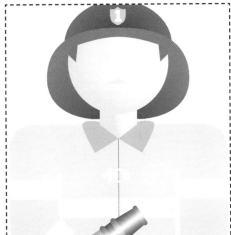

Lesson 46: Changing and Rearranging

 **Overview**

In this lesson the students are helped to see the importance of choosing a career that matches our interests and skills. They also learn that sometimes adults have more than one job in their adult life as they continue to explore the world of work.

 **Grade Level**

2nd

 **Materials**

- *How Santa Got His Job* by Stephen Krensky

 **Time Needed**

30 minutes

 **Objectives**

- Students will learn the hand sign for work.
- Students will hear the story of Santa's journey finding his special job.
- Students will understand the connection of skills and interests to a career.

 **Procedures**

- Teach students the hand sign for work.
- Discuss briefly how many options there are to do in the world and how much time they have to make their decision. Ask them if they knew that many people have more than one job in their adult life. Discuss why this is so.
- Tell them that today we are going to hear a fun story about someone they have all heard of who went through different jobs before he found the one for him. Ask them to try to remember as many of the different jobs he had as they can.
- Read *How Santa Got His Job*. When finished put a list on the board of jobs Santa tried, and why they didn't work for him. Let the students help you fill in the blanks. Tell them that we find our work by knowing ourselves and what we are good at and what we like to do. Ask, "Was Santa good at everything?" "Is anyone?" "Are we good at all the same things as our friends?" "Will we want to do just what our best friend wants to do someday?"

- Emphasize these points as you discuss the book with the students:
  - Santa built on his skills, and kept learning about what he could do.
  - Santa got his final job through trying, having problems, and moving on.
  - Santa didn't give up, he persevered.
  - Santa combined many of his interests and skills in his job.
- Remind students that none of Santa's jobs was a waste, he let each job be an opportunity to learn something. Every job is important and it takes all kinds of people to do the many different jobs there are to be done.
- Close with review of the hand sign for work, and encourage children to continue working hard in the job they have now, school! This is one job you cannot change if you are going to be successful in the world of work some day!

☞ Discussion Questions

- How did Santa find the best job for him?
- What part did a good attitude play in Santa's hunt for a job?
- Which of Santa's different jobs interests you?

☞ Variations

- Using pictures or posters of different jobs, ask students what interests and skills you would need to be successful in each one.
- Let students move around the room, standing in front of different career posters you have placed in different sections of the classroom that interest them. Point out that it is all right to stand in front of more than one, because you have a lot of time before you need to decide.

Lesson 47: It's Not Work, It's My Hobby

👉 Overview

In this lesson students learn the importance of enjoying many hobbies as they grow up, because some day a hobby may become a career. They also learn some new information about some of their classmates as they share hobbies with each other.

👉 Grade Level

3rd

👉 Materials

- Index cards for small group work

👉 Time Needed

30 minutes

👉 Objectives

- Students will learn the hand sign for work.
- Students will realize the connection between hobbies and careers.
- Students will explore jobs that connect with certain hobbies.

👉 Procedures

- Ask students what a hobby is. Get ideas, then divide them into 4 small groups and ask them to come up with at least ten hobbies 3rd graders have. These can be theirs or someone else's they have observed.
- After 5-8 minutes in their small groups bring students back together and have one student from each group list their group's ten hobbies on the board. Compile a class list, not including duplicates.
- Add the following if no one suggests them: reading, doing math puzzles, singing, helping others, playing a sport, building models, baking or cooking, sewing, planting and tending a vegetable garden, planting and tending a flower garden, traveling, writing poetry, acting or singing in a play, drawing, painting, designing scenery for a play, video games, running, babysitting

- Teach students the hand sign for work. Ask them if any of the hobbies they have listed would be considered work. Discuss the fact that doing something we like to do, want to do, and are good at doing doesn't feel like work, and that is what you hope for them when they grow up. You would love for them to find a job that almost feels like a hobby to them.
- Put them back into their small groups and ask each group to take their same ten hobbies and figure out a career that would relate to that hobby.
- Regroup class and have a student report from each small group. As they tell you a career write it next to the hobby on the board or overhead. Allow time for discussion including points such as: some hobbies go with more than one job, some hobbies stay hobbies your whole life even though your job may be different, some hobbies change as we continue to grow up, hobbies can be enjoyed by boys and girls equally, just as jobs can.
- Conclude lesson with summary concept that as we get to know ourselves and what we like to do we will have a better idea of what we would enjoy as a job someday. Review the hand sign for work.

☞ Discussion Questions

- Did any of the hobby/job connections surprise you?
- Do you know anyone whose job used to be their hobby? Tell us about him or her.
- Which hobbies were hard to fit with jobs? Why do you think that is?

☞ Variations

- Add careers the students did not think of and explain what they are. Let the students figure out what hobbies would help a person succeed in that career.
- Give students the homework assignment to find the most unusual hobbies they can by interviewing adults and older students they know. Conduct a class discussion on what careers could connect with these unusual hobbies.

Lesson 48: Pizza Party

☞ Overview

Using a game format, the students learn the career cluster concept. They enjoy matching certain careers with a particular cluster as they play.

☞ Grade Level

4th

☞ Materials

- 5 Pizza Party game boards (see page 168) copied onto construction paper
- 5 sets of "Pizza Toppings Career Titles" on p. 169 copied, cut apart and put in envelopes or plastic bags

☞ Time Needed

30 minutes

☞ Objectives

- Students will learn the hand sign for work.
- Students will be introduced to Holland's Career Clusters.
- Students will recognize sample careers in all six clusters.

☞ Procedures

- Teach the hand sign for work. Relate this to the word career, and discuss the difference in the two words. Lead a short discussion on the importance of knowing the many options for careers available and which ones interest us so that we can learn more about them as we grow. Explain the connection between the world of adult work and the world of being a student, which is their work at this time.
- Talk about the word "cluster" and give examples of things that are grouped in clusters such as grapes, berries, etc.
- Tell students that today we are going to play a game using six career clusters to help us learn the different types of careers and some specific examples in

each cluster. Using the children's models of Holland's Career Clusters on p. 166 explain the six clusters: People (Social), Science (Investigative), Business (Enterprising), Technical and Tools (Realistic), Office (Conventional), and Arts (Artistic). Give a few examples of careers in each cluster as you explain them.

- Divide the class into 4-5 small groups and give each group a Pizza Game Board.
- Distribute a set of the "Pizza Toppings Career Titles" to each small group. Instruct each group to put each career topping on the appropriate space on the game board. As groups work together walk around coaching them, helping them understand that there may be more than one "correct" space for a certain career.
- When all groups are finished, discuss as a whole class the decisions they made, making sure they understand the different careers and cluster concept.
- Tell students that in the fifth grade lesson on careers you will mention these clusters again in more detail but you wanted them to be introduced to them this year.
- Give additional small group time to tell which cluster looks most interesting to them at this time, and why. Point out that as they continue to grow, mature, and experience new places and people, they may find their career cluster interests changing as well. That is what you hope for them, that they will continue to learn about the many options open to them.
- Close lesson with a review of the hand sign for work.

☞ Discussion Questions

- Are there certain clusters for boys and certain ones for girls? Why not?
- Can someone be interested in more than one cluster?
- What kinds of experiences might cause your career interests to change as you grow up?

☞ Variations

- Bring in a few pizzas to celebrate the many career options students have.
- Call out the different clusters and have students stand when you call out the one(s) they are interested in. Discuss the variety and diversity in the class.
- Group students interested in the same cluster together for a short sharing time of jobs in that cluster they are interested in.

CAREER AWARENESS

✎ Lesson 48: Pizza Party

HOLLAND'S CAREER CLUSTERS

People: Teacher, Counselor, Preacher, Childcare Worker, Physical Therapist, Social Worker, Coach, Athletic Trainer, Fund Raiser

Science: Astronomer, Scientist, Doctor, Pharmacist, Computer Programmer, Veterinarian, Mathematician, Chemist, Chiropractor

Business: Real Estate Sales Agent, Cosmetologist, Flight Attendant, Waiter or Waitress, Lawyer, TV or Radio Announcer, Contractor, Claims Adjuster, Insurance Agent, Restaurant Manager

✎ Lesson 48: Pizza Party

HOLLAND'S CAREER CLUSTERS

Technical and Tools: Farmer, Forester, Fire Fighter, Police Officer, Engineer, Mechanic, Chef, Baker, Carpenter, Brick Layer, Yard Maintenance, Soldier, Electrician

Office: Loan Officer, Bank Teller, Hotel Desk Clerk, Receptionist, Secretary, Computer Operator, Mail Carrier, Auditor, Clerk

Arts: Writer, Composer Artist, Decorator, Dancer, Designer, Landscape Architect, Photographer, Architect, Seamstress, Dance Instructor

✎ Lesson 48: Pizza Party

✂ Activity

Directions: Copy onto card stock and cut apart. Give one to each small group for game.

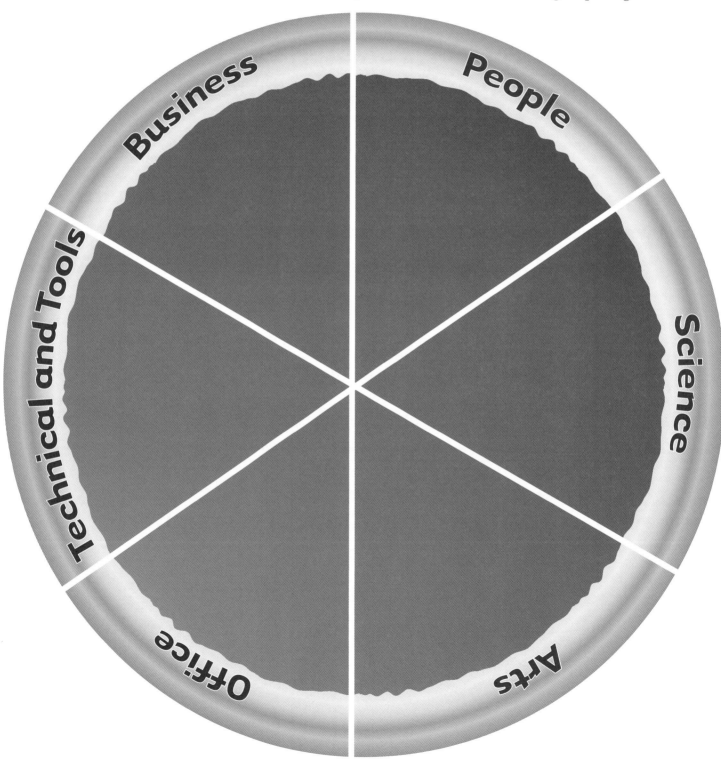

✎ Lesson 48: Pizza Party

✂ Activity

Directions: Copy and cut out, giving a set of all the career titles to each small group in the game.

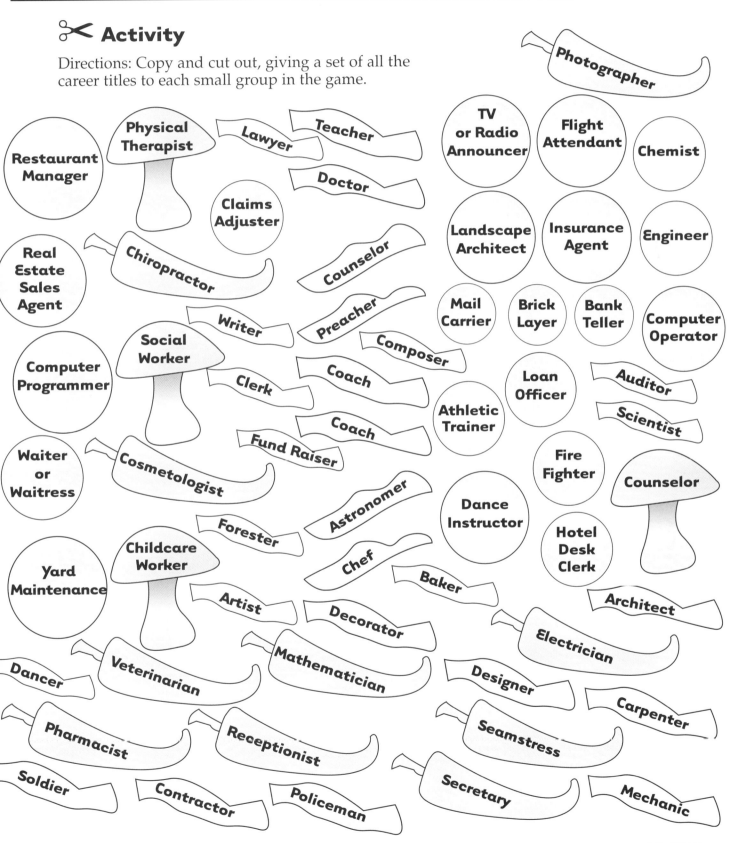

Photographer

Restaurant Manager

Physical Therapist

Lawyer

Teacher

Doctor

Claims Adjuster

TV or Radio Announcer

Flight Attendant

Chemist

Real Estate Sales Agent

Chiropractor

Counselor

Landscape Architect

Insurance Agent

Engineer

Writer

Preacher

Mail Carrier

Brick Layer

Bank Teller

Computer Operator

Social Worker

Composer

Computer Programmer

Clerk

Coach

Loan Officer

Auditor

Scientist

Athletic Trainer

Waiter or Waitress

Cosmetologist

Coach

Fund Raiser

Fire Fighter

Counselor

Forester

Astronomer

Dance Instructor

Childcare Worker

Chef

Baker

Hotel Desk Clerk

Architect

Yard Maintenance

Artist

Decorator

Electrician

Dancer

Veterinarian

Mathematician

Designer

Carpenter

Pharmacist

Receptionist

Seamstress

Soldier

Contractor

Policeman

Secretary

Mechanic

169

© YouthLight Inc.

Lesson 49: Pickin' and Grinnin'

☞ Overview

In this lesson the students learn more about the career cluster concept. They work together in groups researching different careers and discovering which cluster(s) they are most interested in at this time in their lives.

☞ Grade Level

5th

☞ Materials

- Six posters of grape clusters, each with one of the following labels: Social,
- Investigative, Enterprising, Realistic, Conventional, and Artistic
- Copy for each student of the "Career Cluster Worksheet"
- Classroom set of Parramore, Hopke, and Drier. Children's Dictionary of Occupations. (Meridian, 2004).

☞ Time Needed

30 minutes

☞ Objectives

- Students will learn the hand sign for work.
- Students will understand the relationship between their unique personalities and a career choice.
- Students will understand Holland's Six Career Clusters.

☞ Procedures

- Teach students the hand sign for work. Lead a discussion on what they know about work, and if they have ever thought about what they would enjoy and be good at doing. You can expect many of them to have ideas, so it is good to hear these, encourage these dreams, and tell them to keep their options open to new ideas as they continue through school.
- Put words "personality" and "cluster" on the board. Ask them to define these words. Illustrate the word cluster with how grapes are grown. Put up the six grape clusters representing Holland's six career clusters, and tell the students

these clusters represent six personality types that go with certain careers. Tell them that if we find a career that fits our personality we will be happier and more successful. Ask them, "Why would someone pick a career that does not fit their personality?" Encourage answers such as, "That is what someone else wants them to do; it pays more money than what they really want to do, they think it sounds more exciting, etc." Help them understand that others' expectations, money, and assumptions about a job are not the best reasons to choose a career for ourselves. These things are important, but not the most important. Tell them the most important factor in choosing a job is finding one in which you are suited, interested, and excited about so that you can get up every morning looking forward to doing what you like to do.

- Teach the six clusters to the students, going over the personality traits of each. Include in your instruction questions such as, "Are certain clusters just for boys and others just for girls? Why or why not?" "Could you see yourself in more than one cluster?" "Are the cluster(s) you are interested in going to be the same as your best friend's?" Allow a short discussion on these issues.
- Divide class into small groups, making sure each group or student has a copy of the Children's Dictionary of Occupations or another such publication. Give each student a work sheet and ask them to look up some of the possible careers listed in each cluster and discuss them. When you call time each student will fill in the bottom section of their work sheet indicating two clusters they think sound like them, and two careers in each cluster.
- Tell students that you have included a letter to their parents on the back side of this work sheet. Ask them to show their parents the work sheet, the letter, and their answers about their own career interests at this time.
- Close by repeating the hand sign for work. Emphasize the importance of the relationship between what we are interested in, are good at, and what we may choose to do in our lives.

☞ Discussion Questions

- Can you think of a career that you don't think fits into any of the six clusters?
- Do you think the careers you are considering for your future are similar to the ones your parents thought about? Why or why not?
- What careers do you think are available for men and women today that were only for one gender or the other 20 years ago?

☞ Variations

- Play a game called, "Find the cluster." Put the six career cluster names up around the room, call out a career, and have the student whose turn it is stand in front of one cluster and explain why they chose that one.
- Group students according to the cluster they are most interested in at this time. Encourage discussion among them as to why that cluster interests them and what careers in particular they find engaging.

Lesson 49: Career Clusters Worksheet

Dear Parents,

I thought you would be interested in the Career Awareness lesson I led in your child's class this week.

On the other side of this letter is the worksheet your child completed as he or she looked through the Children's Dictionary of Occupations. My goals were to help them explor some of the many choices of careers they have, and to understand that we are happiest in a career that matches our interests and personalities. The students listed two career clusters that they feel fit their personalities as well as some specific jobs in each cluster.

At this stage of development we do not want children to "choose" their future career, but to start exploring their options and getting ideas for their futures. They do not need to be limited at this age, but see the work of work as a wide open field of exciting choices!

Please look over the worksheet with your child. You can certainly call me if you have any questions. The years ahead are full of opportunities for your child to explore career options and learn about the adult world of work. I hope you can enjoy this exploration with him or her. Thank you for your support.

Lesson 49: Career Clusters Worksheet

_____'S CAREER CLUSTERS WORKSHEET

PERSONALITY TYPE CLUSTERS	TRAITS	POSSIBLE CAREERS
SOCIAL	Cooperative, Kind, Generous, Friendly, Cares about Others	Teacher, Counselor, Preacher, Child care Worker, Physical Therapist, Social Worker
INVESTIGATIVE	Independent, Confident, Likes School, Scientific, Self-Motivated	Astronomer, Scientist, Doctor, Pharmacist, Computer Programmer, Veterinarian, Mathematician
ENTERPRISING	Talkative, Likes to Sell Things and Ideas, Witty, Aggressive, Energetic	Real Estate Sales Agent, Cosmetologist, Flight Attendant, Waiter or Waitress, Lawyer, TV or Radio Announcer
REALISTIC	Practical, Reliable, Likes Fixing Things, Mechanical	Farmer, Forester, Fire Fighter, Policeman, Engineer, Mechanic, Chef, Baker
CONVENTIONAL	Orderly, Precise, Careful, Controlled, Careful with Money	Loan Officer, Bank Teller, Hotel Desk Clerk, Receptionist, Secretary, Computer Operator, Mail Carrier
ARTISTIC	Creative, Independent, Free-Spirited, Expressive, Sensitive	Writer, Composer, Artist, Decorator, Dancer Designer, Landscape Architect

In the spaces below write two clusters that describe your personality, and two careers in each cluster that look interesting to you:

Two clusters I think sound like me are: _____ and _____

Two careers in Cluster #1 that interest me are: _____ and _____

Two careers in Cluster #2 that interest me are: _____ and _____

Dear Parents,

All children have dreams of what they want to be when they grow up. Today your child's classroom guidance lesson was on career awareness. We learned the hand sign for work. The goals for career education in the elementary grades are to make children aware of the many options they have, to develop an awareness of the world outside school, and to learn that one's strengths and interests can fit into a career that challenges, fulfills, and interests us.

We have fun with these lessons as we explore various jobs. Children enjoy seeing that in today's world men and women are free to choose many careers, and that the job market continually changes and evolves. You can help with this awareness and exploration as your child grows by pointing out careers in your family, neighborhood, and community as you observe them with your child. You can also help your child become aware of his or her strengths, talents, and interests and look for particular careers that match their personalities.

Sincerely,

Your School Counselor

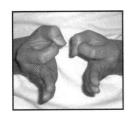

DECISIONS AND CONSEQUENCES

All of us are faced with choices and decisions every day, and children are no exception. Many times, however, they have not yet learned that many of these choices are not automatic, and can involve their thinking as well as their impulses. Of course, this is a developmental issue as well, and depending on the age of the child we can expect more or less thought to go into a decision. Young children are ready, however, for lessons which show them that what we do and say have consequences, and that part of growing up is learning to stop and think about what will happen before we do something which could harm us or someone else. The following lessons help students see this relationship, give them opportunities to think through actions, and have fun learning the importance of making good choices and decisions.

☞ Hand Sign* for this lesson:

__DECISION__ Hold left hand in front of body with thumb and index finger making a circle, other three fingers extended. With right hand near forehead, point index finger on forehead then pull right hand down in front of body. End with palms facing each other and right hand just like left, with thumb and index finger making a circle and other three fingers extended.

*Adapted from Costello, Elaine. Concise American Sign Language Dictionary. Random House. 2000.

Lesson 50: 1 Little, 2 Little, 3 Little

☞ Overview

This lesson introduces to young children the concept of making decisions. They learn that there are some decisions they can make for themselves, and others that require adult help.

☞ Grade Level

Pre-K

☞ Materials

- Three markers or crayons in different colors
- Three classroom games from the shelves
- Three children's books
- Three different puzzles
- Three different puppets
- Three toys from a housekeeping center in the classroom
- Three different sized balls

☞ Time Needed

20 minutes

☞ Objectives

- Children will learn the hand sign for decision.
- Children will practice making simple choices.
- Children will understand they can make choices all by themselves.

☞ Procedures

- Teach the hand sign for decision. Ask children what they think this word means and allow time for a short discussion.
- Taking one set of three items at a time, lay them out in front of you on the floor for all the children to see. Bring up three children at a time, and ask

them to choose one of the items from the set. Work with the children as they choose, helping them process with the following questions:
- Will each of us make the same decision?
- Is one decision better than another?
- Is it hard to make a decision?
- What should we do if someone else decides the same thing we do?
- Do we make the same choice every time?

- Teach the following song to tune of "One Little, Two Little, Three Little Indians."

> One little, two little, three little decisions
> Four little, five little, six little decisions,
> Seven little, eight little, nine little decisions
> We make decisions every day!

- As you sing you can put up nine fingers and clap on last word of the song. Tell children that as they grow they will keep making decisions, some will be easy and some will be hard. They will always have caring adults to help them if they need it, but some decisions they can make all by themselves, just like today.
- Review the hand sign for decision.

☞ Discussion Questions

- Can you think of a decision you have made so far today that you are proud of?
- What should you do if you make a decision that gets you in trouble?
- Do you think adults sometimes make decisions that they wish they could change?

☞ Variations

- Make a class bulletin board with pictures the children have drawn of themselves making a good decision. Label it, and read the label to the class before putting the picture on the board.
- Tell an ongoing story that allows the children to make the decision when the main character can't decide what to do. For example, "Once upon a time there was a little boy who didn't know if he should share his toy with his friend." The children decide what he should do, then the teacher continues taking the boy through the day and letting the children make different decisions for him. This helps them to see how many decisions they are in the position to make every day.

Lesson 51: Dollar, Dollar, Who's Got The Dollar?

☞ Overview

This lesson helps young children understand the correlation between making a decision and the consequences of that decision. As they help their puppet friend with a dilemma, they see that the different decisions she could make have different consequences.

☞ Grade Level

Kindergarten

☞ Materials

- Large Puppet with one dollar bill taped to her/his hand

☞ Time Needed

20 minutes

☞ Objectives

- Students will learn the hand sign for decision.
- Students will identify a variety of decisions they can make.
- Students will understand the relationship between a decision and its consequences.

☞ Procedures

- As you enter the room, children will notice the dollar bill taped to the hand of the puppet. When they ask about it, tell them you will let the puppet tell them about it after you have taught them the hand signs for today's lesson.
- Teach hand sign for decision. Discuss this sign, making sure you point out that to make a good decision you use your mind and think about it. Tell them we will talk more about this later, but the puppet is ready to tell you about the money she found. (While you are talking about today's hand sign, the puppet is acting very restless, obviously excited about what she has to tell the children.)
- The puppet tells the children that she found this dollar in the hall as she came to school today. She knows just what she can do with it, buy some candy! She can't wait until school is over so she can spend the money.

- Tell the children that we can use this situation to talk about today's word – decision. Ask them if the puppet has any other choice of what to do with the money besides spend it. Allow them time to think about it and give you some options. At the end of the discussion review the options the children have mentioned. Make sure you include these: puppet could keep it and spend it later; puppet could save it; puppet could take it to office and give it to the secretary telling her she found it in the hall.
- Tell children that now we are going to think about what would happen depending on which decision she makes. Tell them this is called a consequence, what happens. Allow the class to come up with ideas, summing them up as follows:
  - Spends it for candy.....eats candy, money is gone, owner never gets it back
  - Saves money.....money still around, owner never gets it back
  - Takes money to office.....owner may claim it, or puppet may get it later if no one claims it
- Ask class which decision they think is the right one. As they talk help them understand that just because we find something it doesn't make it ours. Give them some possible scenarios as to who may be the rightful owner of the dollar – a child who is paying for lunch or snack, a parent who was bringing it to pay for school pictures, a teacher who had just received change from the office for supplies for her class, etc.
- Tell students that choices and decisions are like this, whatever we decide has consequences, things that happen depending on what we do. Give them some additional examples to help you with, for example: you want to be first but someone else got there ahead of you; you want to keep swinging but someone else is waiting for a turn; you want to call someone a name because they made you so mad.
- Bring puppet back out and ask her what she is going to do with the money now that she realizes there are consequences to what decision we make. Let her tell the class that she is going to turn it in since it really isn't hers. She is going to tell her mom what she did and maybe her mom will let her have some candy today anyway.
- Review the hand sign for decision.

☞ Discussion Questions

- Have you ever found something that was not yours? What did you do with it?
- Has anyone ever returned something of yours that they found? How did that make you feel?
- Who could you ask to help you with your decision if you couldn't decide what to do?

☞ Variations

- Continue to point out good and not so good consequences of decisions that children make as they go through their day in the classroom.
- Invite parents to write the class a short paragraph or two about a decision they made and the consequences that went with it. This will help the children see that even adults continue to deal with the consequences of their decisions.

Lesson 52: So Now What Happens?

☞ Overview

This lesson uses interactive role play situations to engage the children. Their participation will increase their understanding of decision-making and the consequences that follow each decision.

☞ Grade Level

1st

☞ Materials

- Balloon
- Breakable object
- Copy of the "Smiley and Sad Faces" on p. 183 for each student

☞ Time Needed

30 minutes

☞ Objectives

- Students will learn the hand sign for decision.
- Students will develop their understanding of decisions and consequences.
- Students will recognize how many decisions they make for themselves.

☞ Procedures

- Teach the hand sign for decision. Discuss with the children what this word means. Introduce the word consequences, explaining it means what happens after you decide something.
- Blow up the balloon. Ask children what would happen if we decided to sit on it. Demonstrate by sitting on it and letting it pop. Explain to class that the balloon popping is the consequence of deciding to sit on it. Hold up a breakable object and ask them what would happen if you decided to drop it. Breaking the object would be the consequence of making that decision. (You do not need to show this consequence.)

- Tell students that today we will practice making decisions and learn how some decisions have good consequences and some have bad consequences. Some decisions help us and some give us problems. Give out a smiley and sad face to each student.
- Ask for volunteers, and enact the following role plays with them. You will talk through the role play as the child or children "act" it out. (Engaging in role plays helps keep the children's' attention, and when they participate they learn more.) As role plays are acted out, ask children to hold up either a Smiley Face (for a happy consequence) or a Sad Face (for an unhappy consequence). Ask the children why this would be a good or a bad consequence as you look at which face they have held up.

Role Plays

You borrow a crayon from a friend and enjoy coloring a picture. When you finish and are putting the crayons back in the box, you accidentally break one. You don't tell your friend, and return the crayons quietly.

You are working on your homework and see that it is time for your favorite show on TV. You decide to tell your parents you are finished so you can watch it, even though you are not.

Two of your friends and you are walking down the hall. You are the only ones in the hall. Your friends start to run and yell at you to follow them, so you start running too.

Your ball goes into the street, and you decide to get your parent to get it rather than chasing it yourself.

You see some other kids throwing rocks at recess. They ask you to join them, but you tell them you have to go to the bathroom, and run the other way.

You are in line at lunch. Another student pushes you out of the way and gets in line in front of you. You push him back and holler at him.

Your teacher sends you into the room to get her gloves off her desk during recess. You are the only one in the building since everyone else is outside. You see a pretty pen you would love to have, but it is the teacher's. You get the gloves and quickly go back outside.

You notice some kids calling the new student some ugly names. You walk the other way, and pretend you didn't notice.

You see an older kid offer a younger one a cigarette on the bus. You decide to tell your parents about it when you get home.

- As the children are performing the role plays, ask them what would happen if the student did something else? Give them time to process each situation. It is

Lesson 52: So Now What Happens?

important to make certain the children realize they always have options, and that there are many good decisions that can be made. It is also important to remind them that adults are there to help them if they will let them know they need help.

- Close the lesson with a review of the hand sign for decision, and the meaning of the word consequence.

☞ Discussion Questions

- Why is it sometimes hard to make a good decision?
- Is it easier to make a good decision when you are alone or when you are with someone else? Why do you think this is?
- Give us an example of both a good and a bad consequence to a decision you have made. What did you learn after making that decision?

☞ Variations

- After the students have acted out a few of the role plays listed, ask them if they can think of a situation they would like to act out. After you have listened to the suggestion, and if it is appropriate, give the student the opportunity to role play it.
- Help students make a list of the trusted adults they can go to in different settings if they need help in making a good decision.

Lesson 52: Smiley and Sad Faces

✂ Activity

Directions:
Copy on card
stock, laminate,
and give to
each student
to use in role
plays.

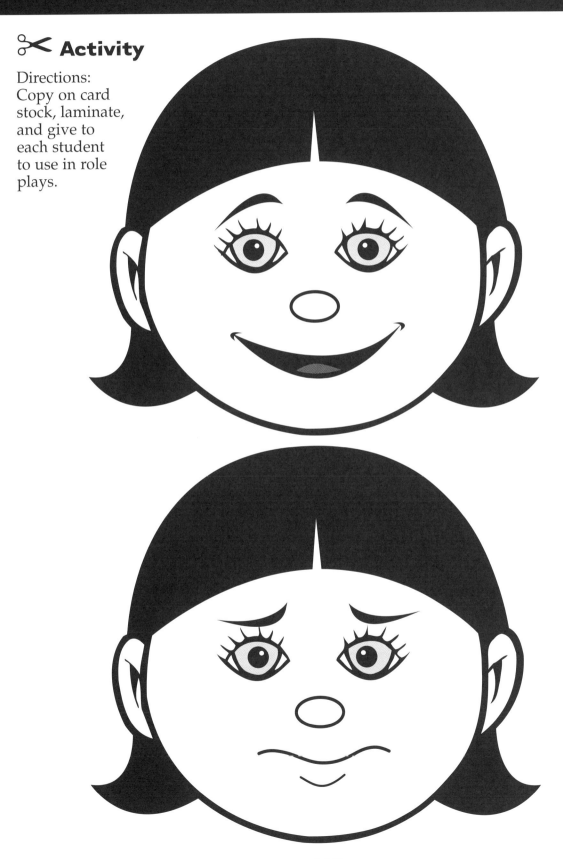

183

Lesson 53: Flies in a Pie

 ## Overview

This lesson engages the students as the counselor is entering the room. As the lesson progresses he/she engages the children in further awareness of the choices we all make every day, consciously or unconsciously, and the consequences that follow.

 ## Grade Level

2nd

Materials

- *Franklin Fibs* by Paulette Bourgeois and Brenda Clark
- Copy of "My Fly Pie" picture on p. 185 for each student

 ## Time Needed

30 minutes

Objectives

- Students will learn the hand sign for decision.
- Students will understand the relationship between making a decision and the subsequent consequences.
- Students will recognize their ability to make thoughtful decisions.

Procedures

- As you enter the classroom, finish eating a piece of candy and drop the wrapper on the floor instead of in the trashcan. As the students continue to watch you get ready for the lesson, pick up a pencil from a child's desk, say, "I like this pencil, I think I'll use it." Then put it with the other materials you have. Before you greet the children, pick up a book from the teacher's desk, look through it, and put it back in a different place.
- Greet the students, telling them that today we are going to talk about making decisions, and what happens after we do. Write the two words on the board – DECISION and CONSEQUENCES and discuss their meanings.

- Ask them if they noticed you making any decisions on what you did as you came into the room today. They will probably tell you the three things you did. In the discussion make the following points:
  - You chose to drop the candy wrapper, you could just as easily put it in the trash. What are the consequences of this decision?
  - You chose to pick up the child's pencil and not to ask to borrow it. What are consequences of this decision?
  - You chose to look at the book on the teacher's desk and move it somewhere else. What are consequences of this decision?
- Tell students that we make many decisions that we never think about, we just do things. Part of growing up is learning to use our brains along with our bodies as we go through the day. Teach the hand sign for decision, and point out to them that this sign shows a connection between your brain and your hands.
- Explain to the students that we make decisions as to what we say as well as what we do, and we are going to read a story about a little turtle, Franklin, who makes such a choice. Ask them to listen carefully to what Franklin decides to tell his friends, and the consequences of his decision.
- Read book to students. Engage them in a discussion using the following as a guide:
  - Why did Franklin decide to lie to his friends about what he could do?
    They were bragging and he wanted to be able to do something special too.
  - What were some of the consequences of his decision to lie?
    He could not eat, sleep, think of anything else. His friends laughed at him, and knew he had told a fib. If he had not told the truth he might have stopped playing with them and become very lonely.
  - How did Franklin get out of the mess his lie got him into?
    He told the truth, then thought of a way he could eat that many flies – in a pie!
  - How did the story end?
    It ended happily with all the friends playing together again.
  - How would the story have ended if Franklin had not made the decision to tell the truth?
    He would have been lonely and his friends could not have trusted him.
- Distribute the "My Fly Pie" pictures, and instruct students to write a good decision they have made on each of the flies. Help them get started with suggestions on the board such as: told my parents the truth when I left the milk on the counter, asked a friend to join the rest of us in a game, loaned my pencil to a friend who needed one, did my work slowly and neatly, finished my homework by myself, etc.
- Before you leave, make sure you pick up the candy wrapper, return the pencil to the student apologizing for taking it, and put the teacher's book back where it was. Tell students that most of the time when we make a bad decision we can apologize and make a better one. This is called learning from our mistakes, and it shows we are growing up, just like Franklin.
- Review the hand sign for today's lesson in closing.

Lesson 53: Flies in a Pie

☞ Discussion Questions

- Ask students, "What did you think when I entered the room and tossed my wrapper on the floor, picked up someone else's pencil, and took a book from the teacher's desk?" "Why do you think I did those things?"
- Have you ever wanted to lie to your friends like Franklin because you were embarrassed about not being able to do something? Do you think all of us feel that way sometimes?
- What else could Franklin have done from the very beginning of the story?

☞ Variations

- Let a student simulate coming into the classroom in the morning and let the class observe all the choices he/she makes that he/she is not even aware of. For example: Does he put his homework where the teacher wants it? Does she smile at a classmate? Does he stop by a friend's desk or go straight to his own? Does she hang her jacket where it is supposed to go or just toss it in the cubby?
- Send their fly pies home for parents to see and sign, to encourage good decision making. Make a class bulletin board of these pies and have a party, serving fly pie made with raisins instead of flies!

✎ Lesson 53: My Fly Pie

✄ Activity

Directions: Copy for each student and ask them to write a decision they have made today on each fly.

Lesson 54: What Time Is It?

 Overview

This lesson increases children's awareness of the many decisions they make every day, all day long. As they process some of their decisions they gain understanding of how important it is to make decisions that have good, healthy consequences.

 Grade Level

3rd

 Materials

- Copy of clock pattern on the following page for each student

 Time Needed

30 minutes

 Objectives

- Students will learn the hand sign for decision.
- Students will recognize how many decisions they make every day.
- Students will relate consequences to decisions made.

 Procedures

- Teach students the hand sign for lesson. Discuss the significance of the sign for including the brain as well as the hands. Ask students why they think this is.
- Ask students how many decisions they make every day. After a few responses, tell them that today we are going to write down some of those decisions and think about what happens to us when we make certain decisions.
- Put the word "consequence" on the board and discuss its meaning in relationship to making decisions. Make sure students understand that consequences can be both good and bad, depending on the decision made. Give examples of each.
- Distribute the students' clocks. Point out that there are two clocks, a morning one and an evening one.

- Starting with 7:00 AM, help the students fill in a few of the blocks together. When you think they are ready, ask them to continue going through their days, putting one decision per hour. As they work walk around the room helping as needed. Remind students that they are choosing only one decision out of many per hour, so to think about one they remember as being important to them.
- When all are finished, engage students in a class discussion asking:
  - Which decisions were the easiest for you? Why?
  - Which were the hardest? Why?
  - Are you surprised at how many decisions you make all by yourself every day?
  - Were any of your decisions influenced by other people, like friends, teachers, or parents?
  - Do you like making decisions or does it bother you or worry you?
  - Were the consequences of your decisions good ones for the most part?
  - Would you make a different decision at any time if you could go back and do it again? Why or why not?
- Review the hand sign and encourage students to remember how many decisions they can make for themselves and how important it is to make decisions that have good, positive consequences.

☞ Discussion Questions

- Do all people find the same decisions difficult or easy? Why do you think this is?
- What do you think about when you are trying to make a good decision?
- How does it feel to know that you are in control of so many decisions every day?

☞ Variations

- Put students in small groups to share their individual decision clocks with each other before leading a class discussion.
- Put up a poster of a large clock in the classroom and let the students write good decisions they have made on it as the day goes on. The teacher could also write these decisions as he or she sees them being made.

✎ Lesson 54: Morning Decision Clock

✂ Activity

Directions: Write one decision per hour you might make starting at 7:00 AM.

✎ Lesson 54: Evening Decision Clock

✂ Activity

Directions: Write one decision per hour you might make starting at 12:00 PM.

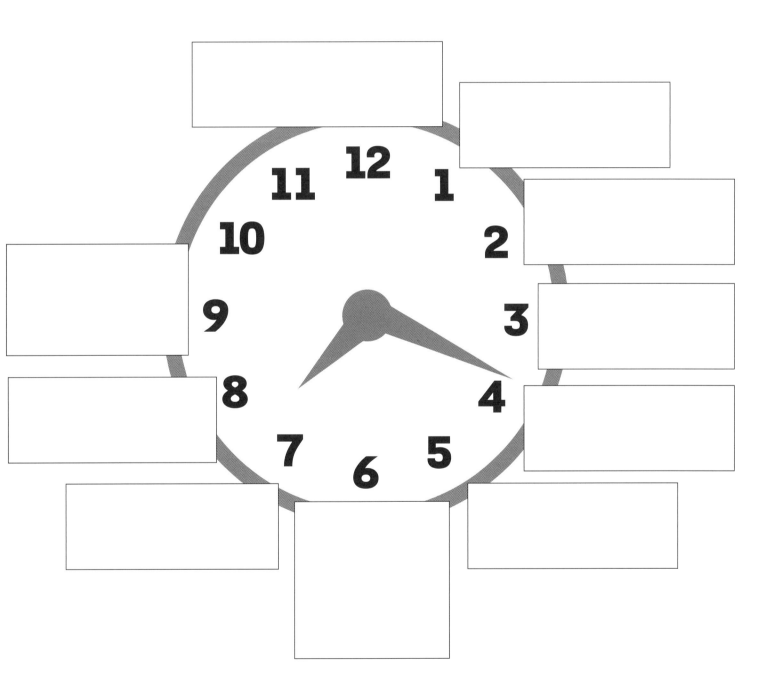

Lesson 55: Risky Business

 Overview

During this lesson students become more aware of the element of risk in making certain decisions. As they play a classroom game they increase their understanding of thoughtful vs. impulsive decision making.

 Grade Level

4th

☞ **Materials**

- Long narrow strip of bulletin board paper labeled "The Edge of the Cliff"
- Copy and cut apart set of "Risky Business Cards"
- 20 "stepping stones" made of cut up poster board or construction paper

☞ **Time Needed**

30 minutes

☞ **Objectives**

- Students will learn the hand sign for decision.
- Students will understand risk factors involved in certain decisions.
- Students will explore the difference between wise and unwise risks.

☞ **Procedures**

- Teach students the hand sign for the lesson. Discuss the significance of the connection of the brain to the hands. Emphasize that part of growing up is showing you can use your brain and think when you make decisions. Remind them how babies do everything impulsively, but as children continue to mature and grow they use their heads more and more.
- Ask them to define "risk." Include the point that some risks are healthy and good for us and some are dangerous and unsafe.
- Announce that today we are going to play a game to help us see the relationship between making good decisions while using our brains and making impulsive decisions that can be dangerous for us and/or others.

- Divide the class into two teams. Put a long piece of bulletin board paper which you have labeled "The Edge of the Cliff" on the floor in the front of the room. Put the 2 sets of 10 "stepping stones" side by side leading up to the edge of the cliff. One team will use one path of stones, and the other team the other path. Ask the first student on each team to stand on the first stepping stone on each path toward cliff. Taking turns, each student will draw a card from the stack of cards you have brought. The student will read the decision out loud and take that many steps either closer to or further away from the cliff. (The card will indicate if they are to move forward or backward.) If the decision is a positive one the student will move his or her team away from the cliff, if it is a negative or harmful decision the student will move the team's position closer to the cliff. After each student's turn another team member will take the preceding team member's place on the stepping stones and draw the next decision card.
- Continue to play until one team member goes over the cliff. Ask students to tell you what kinds of cliffs people go over in life when they make risky, unhealthy, and unwise decisions. Include in the discussion such cliffs as failing grades, dropping out of school, getting sick, being too unhealthy to be active and energetic, getting addicted to a substance that is harmful, losing a job, losing a friend, etc.
- Ask students why some of the decisions took you two steps closer to the cliff, and some only one. Can they think of any other decisions that are dangerous as well as risky?
- Review the hand sign in closing.

☞ Discussion Questions

- If someone wants to take a risk, what are some safe and healthy ways to do this? (Encourage sports, individual challenges in nature and academics, etc.)
- What could you do if you see a friend making a risky decision that could bring harm to him or her?
- Which is harder, making a risky decision or saying no to one? Why?

☞ Variations

- Point out to students that some of us have more risk-taking personalities than others. Let them group themselves on a continuum from 1 to 10 as to how much of a risk taker they are. Put yourself on the imaginary line at the front of the room first, and explain why you are at that point. This will help them understand what you are asking them to do. As they group themselves encourage them to make individual decisions, not ones like their friends. Encourage a class discussion on the different places we are on the line and why.
- Have students write a letter to a trusted adult, asking that person to warn them if they see them making a risky decision that could cause harm. Help them mail these letters to the parent, grandparent, aunt, uncle, teacher, etc.

Lesson 55: Risky Business Cards

✂ Activity

Directions: Copy these decisions on card stock and cut apart.

Leave homework unfinished (Forward 1)	**Run into the road after a ball (Forward 2)**
Steal a book from the library (Forward 2)	**Tell a lie about another student (Forward 1)**
Eat three candy bars (Forward 1)	**Finish homework (Back 1)**
Learn to play a new sport (Back 1)	**Laugh at yourself when you make a mistake (Back 1)**
Try out for a play (Back 1)	**Tell your friend's secret (Forward 1)**
Ask a friend over to your house (Back 1)	**Help your parents clean up the garage (Back 1)**
Help a younger student in math (Back 1)	**Tell your mother you don't want to help (Forward 1)**
Copy a friend's answers on a test (Forward 1)	**Tell a friend you like her new jeans (Back 1)**
Run in the school halls (Forward 1)	**Pull someone's hair (Forward 1)**
Try a cigarette an older student offers you (Forward 2)	**Hit someone when you are mad (Forward 1)**
Ask the teacher for help (Back 1)	**Laugh at someone else when they make a mistake (Forward 1)**

✎ Lesson 55: Risky Business Cards

✂ Activity

Directions: Copy these decisions on card stock and cut apart.

Take a pill from a friend to see what will happen (Forward 2)	**Use your lunch money for junk food, not lunch (Forward 1)**
Stay up late on a school night (Forward 1)	**Hurry through your work to finish first (Forward 1)**
Laugh when your friend comes in with a new haircut (Forward 1)	**Take your time so that your work is neat and correct (Back 1)**
Tell your friend you like his new haircut (Back 1)	**Tease the new student every day (Forward 1)**
Help your classmate pick up a stack of papers she dropped (Back 1)	**Tell your friend that someone else doesn't like her (Forward 1)**
Roll your eyes at the principal (Forward 1)	**Ask your parent for help with your homework (Back 1)**
Talk back to the teacher (Forward 1)	**Cut your own hair (Forward 1)**
Tell the teacher you don't understand (Back 1)	**Accept a ride with a stranger (Forward 2)**
Ask the teacher for help after school (Back 1)	**Try to drive your parents' car when they are not home (Forward 2)**
Tell your parents you don't have homework when you do (Forward 1)	**Shoplift a candy bar when your friend dares you to (Forward 2)**
Go to bed on time (Back 1)	**Cut your little brother's hair (Forward 1)**

Lesson 56: Shake It Up!

 ## Overview

This lesson gives the students a helpful acronym to use when they are confused about making a decision. Small group work enforces the use of this acronym.

 ## Grade Level

5th

 ## Materials

- Copy of "Shake It Up!" worksheet for each student

 ## Time Needed

30 minutes

 ## Objectives

- Students will learn the hand sign for decision.
- Students will understand the relationship between thinking and decision making.
- Students will discuss the formula for making a hard decision.

Procedures

- Teach class the hand sign for decision. Explain to them the significance of the sign involving the brain as well as the hands.
- Engage class in a discussion about making decisions. Ask them what they think about when they have a hard decision to make. Write responses on the board, making sure they include safety, health, and what is right. Ask them if it is always easy to make the "right" decision. Why or why not?
- Teach them the acronym SHAKE, and explain how it can help them as they are thinking about a hard decision they have to make. Say, "You can ask yourself will this decision have a Safe, Healthy, And Kind Ending? If yes, then that is probably a good decision.
- Divide class into small groups of 3-4 and distribute "Shake It Up" worksheets.

- Allow time to work in groups then let each group report back to the class which decision was the hardest for them, why they think it was hard, and what their group decision was. Give them time to explain if they had a hard time agreeing or not, and how did they resolve the conflict. Make sure you point out that there are multiple decisions that can be made regarding these situations, and all could have healthy, safe and kind consequences or endings.
- Ask each small group to share the fifth decision they thought of that would be hard, and how they would act on it.
- Review the hand sign for decision, encouraging students to remember to think before making a difficult decision, to ask for help if they need it, and to SHAKE it up!

👉 Discussion Questions

- Is it a sign of weakness or strength to ask a trusted adult for help in making an important decision? Why?
- What is one important decision you have made today? Why was it important?
- Are our little decisions as important as the big ones sometimes? Why or why not?

👉 Variations

- Ask students to interview a trusted adult about making decisions. Let them decide what questions to ask but include the following: Do you still have a hard time making decisions, even as an adult? What is one important decision you made and why was it a good one? Can you think of a time when you had to live with the consequences of a bad decision?
- To further reinforce the SHAKE acronym, make students milkshakes. In order to get one each student has to tell one good decision they made that day, and why it was safe, healthy, and kind.

✎ Lesson 56: Shake It Up!

✂ Activity

Directions: Discuss as a small group the following four situations, deciding what you would do. Remember to use our SHAKE code to help you. Add a fifth situation to the list that you would like to share with the class, a decision you may have had to make at one time.

> To make a good decision, ask yourself, "Will it **SHAKE**?
>
> Will it have a **S**afe, **H**ealthy, **A**nd **K**ind **E**nding?
>
> If so, you know what to do!

1. You have finished your homework and you are heading outside to play basketball with some friends. Your little brother wants to come along, and your mom says he can if it is OK with you. What would you do?

2. You are riding home on the bus, and the older student in front of you offers you a cigarette. You tell him you are not interested, but he calls you a baby, and insists you take it. He even puts the cigarette in your lap. What would you do?

3. You see a friend of yours picking on a new classmate, calling her an ugly name. You just ignore it, because you don't want to get involved. Later in the day your friend asks you to go with him or her to tease the new girl some more. What would you do?

4. You are the last one out of the cafeteria at lunch, and find $5 on the floor. You pick it up and really want to keep it. No one saw you, and you could use it for the new video game you are saving to buy. What would you do?

5.

DECISIONS AND CONSEQUENCES

✎ Lesson 56: Shake It Up!

✂ Activity

Directions: Create five situations to discuss as a small group, deciding what you would do. Remember to use our SHAKE code to help you.

> To make a good decision, ask yourself, "Will it **SHAKE**?
> Will it have a **S**afe, **H**ealthy, **A**nd **K**ind **E**nding?
> If so, you know what to do!

1. _____

_____

_____

2. _____

_____

_____

3. _____

_____

_____

4. _____

_____

_____

5. _____

_____

_____

199

Dear Parents,

Today's guidance lesson was on making decisions and understanding that decisions come with consequences. Our hand sign was for the word decision. Children are faced with increasingly important decisions as they grow, and school-age children are not too young to begin learning the relationship between what they decide to do or say and what happens next – the consequences. They need to be given the opportunity early in life to make simple decisions for themselves and learn from the consequences- good or bad. When they understand this relationship between making a decision and living with the consequence, they will learn to think through the more difficult decisions facing them as they grow. Some decisions even have risks and the older students played a game to help them understand this concept, and that some decisions can cause them or others harm. As you talk to your child about today's lesson, share with them some easy and not so easy decisions you have made today or recently. Let them share with you some decisions they are proud of, and some they are not. This is a wonderful way to learn about their day, and to share yours with them as well. Discussions like this help us understand our children better, and to know how to help them in this challenging task of growing up.

Sincerely,

Your School Counselor

FEELINGS

Recognition, acceptance, and understanding of our feelings is key to healthy emotional development for all of us. Children need to learn to name, talk about, and handle strong emotions as they occur, so they do not lose control and hurt themselves or others. Most children enter school with a limited feeling vocabulary, but can quickly learn many more words to go with what they are feeling at a particular moment. All children are comforted when they understand their feelings are neither good nor bad, they just are; they are part of being human and everyone has them. The following lessons help students understand this while also recognizing that not all feelings are comfortable and happy. Children can be taught that feelings change quickly, and we can help this by recognizing them and talking about them when appropriate.

☞ Hand Sign* for this lesson:

FEELING   A bent middle finger indicates feeling in sign language. With right hand palm facing in at chest level, bend middle finger and move hand slightly up and down in front of chest.

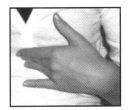

Adapted from Costello, Elaine. Concise American Sign Language Dictionary. Random House. 2000.

Lesson 57: Rocking and Rolling

☞ Overview

The use of a simple trick in this lesson engages the children as they increase their feeling word vocabulary.

☞ Grade Level

Pre-K

☞ Materials

- Crisp brown paper lunch bag
- A book with pictures of children experiencing different feelings, such as:
  Freymann, Saxton and Elffers, Joost, *How Are You Feeling?* Scholastic, 1999.
  Curtis, Jamie Lee. *Today I Feel Silly and Other Moods That Make My Day.*
  Joanna Cotler Books, 1998.
  Cain, Janan. *The Way I Feel.* Parenting Press. 2000.

☞ Time Needed

20 minutes

☞ Objectives

- Students will learn the hand sign for feeling.
- Students will develop a feeling words vocabulary.
- Students will understand we all have different feelings every day.

☞ Procedures

- Teach students the hand sign for feelings. Remind them that our feelings are very important, and change many times during the day. Sometimes we like what we are feeling and sometimes we do not, but we can remember when we are having a feeling we do not like it will not always be with us.
- Read the book you brought, asking children to notice the faces of the characters with the different feelings, and to try to remember as many of the feeling words as they can.
- Bring out the paper bag and tell the children that we are going to pretend we each have a pile of rocks in front of us, and we are going to take turns

throwing a rock into the bag and yelling out a feeling word. (When you "catch" the rocks in your bag you will perform a simple magic trick* that will wow the children and help them pay attention to the words they are saying as they throw).

- Hold the bag at the top with your fingers positioned as they are when you snap them. Your thumb will be on the outside of the top of the bag facing you and your middle finger inside the bag. Your middle finger will be on the other side of your thumb, one inside the bag and one outside. When you pretend to catch the rock snap your fingers and the sound will be like something landing in the bag. The children will love this and all will want to throw a rock. You can embellish this trick by catching the rocks under your leg, pretend that they are bouncing off the ceiling and landing in your bag, whistling as they fall, etc. You will have to practice a little before you do this in class, but the effect is quite effective and fun.

- As they throw they have to continue thinking of feeling words they remember from the book. Help them include all the ones mentioned in the book so that their feeling vocabularies can begin to grow. So that all have a turn you may want to allow the ones who do not get an individual turn to throw all at once on the count of three, yelling out a feeling word as they do.

- When your rock pile is high, remind children that we all have these feelings and they are an important part of who we are.

- Something the children love after this lesson is to whisper to them that we will put the rocks in the teacher's chair but not to tell her, and watch what happens when she sits down. (This will have to be pre-arranged with the teacher of course.) If the teacher is willing to conduct this charade the children love it when she sits on the rocks! Then she can ask them about the lesson and they have an additional opportunity to talk about the new feeling words they have learned.

- As the teacher is sitting on the rocks you are slipping out the door! The children will enjoy this and tell you about it later.

☞ Discussion Questions

- Name some feelings that you like to have.
- Name some feelings you do not like to have.
- Do you think everyone has these different feelings?
- What are some things you can do to help yourself feel better?

☞ Variations

- Have class cut out pictures from magazines of different feelings people have. Construct a class bulletin board with these pictures.
- From time to time during circle time, point out different feelings you see children experiencing. This will help them relate the feeling words to their actual feelings.

*Paper bag trick included in *Mind Bloggers* by Bob Bowman, Youthlight, Inc.

Lesson 58: Guess The Feeling

☞ Overview

This lesson focuses on seven basic feelings that young children have. They learn that not all people have the same feeling about a particular event, and that feelings change frequently.

☞ Grade Level

Kindergarten

☞ Materials

- Copy and cut apart pictures of children with six basic feelings: angry, happy, sad, afraid, excited, proud, on page 206
- Copy and cut apart the "How do I feel?" cards on page 207 and place in basket or bag.

☞ Time Needed

20 minutes

☞ Objectives

- Students will learn the hand sign for feelings.
- Students will identify six basic feelings and the events that can cause them.
- Students will understand the relationship between feelings and events.
- Students will learn not everyone feels the same way about a particular event.

☞ Procedures

- Teach the hand sign for feelings. Say to children, "Our feelings are very important and help make us who we are. We all have feelings, and they change all day long. Today we are going to act out some feelings and see if other students can guess what feeling it is. We are also going to see that not everyone has the same feeling when the same thing happens to them."
- Show pictures of children's faces with five different feelings. Ask children to make similar faces as you hold up the pictures.
- Ask for three volunteers to come stand beside you. Draw a situation out of the basket or bag, whisper it to them, and ask them to freeze their faces and

bodies showing the feeling they would have if this happened to them. Ask class to identify the feelings the three children are showing. Point out if they are all alike or not.

- Tell the students what the event was. Tell them that all of us are different with different feelings, and sometimes you will feel one way and your friend another and that is all right.
- Call three more students to the front until you have given every child a turn who wants one. If there are situations left, call them out and ask the whole class to freeze their faces and bodies showing a particular feeling.
- Review the hand sign in closing.

☞ Discussion Questions

- Can you think of a time when you had more than one feeling at once? Was that confusing? Why or why not?
- Do you think adults have lots of different feelings too? How can you tell?
- Can you feel one way about a situation one day and have a different feeling about the same situation the very next day? Why do you think this happens?

☞ Variations

- Take digital pictures of the children as you see their faces change showing different feelings. After showing them the pictures, make a class collage with them demonstrating the many feelings we each have every day.
- Use the "How Do I Feel" cards for a rainy day game, calling out a situation and asking the whole class to freeze their faces with an appropriate feeling. Make sure the children look around and notice how different children have different feelings regarding the same situation.

✎ Lesson 58: How Do I Feel Cards

✄ Activity

Directions: Copy on card stock and cut out.

Your mother tells you she is signing you up for swimming lessons.	**Your team won a game.**
Your teacher sends you to time out for yelling in class.	**Your team lost a game.**
Your little brother is having a birthday party.	**You fell and skinned your knee.**
Your friend is playing with someone else at recess.	**Your best friend is going to Disney World.**
You are having trouble writing your letters neatly.	**You are going on a roller coaster ride with your parents.**
You have a new babysitter coming tonight.	**It is your turn to bat in t-ball.**
It is your birthday.	**Today is the last day of school.**
Your little sister tore up your homework paper.	**Today is the first day of a new school year.**
Your dog is wagging his tail when you come home.	**A classmate called you a name.**
Your father is taking you to the park.	**A classmate broke in front of you in line.**

FEELINGS

Lesson 58: Feeling Faces

✂ Activity

Directions: Cut out and show to students.

© YouthLight Inc.

Lesson 58: Feeling Faces

✂ Activity

Directions: Cut out and show to students.

✎ Lesson 58: Feeling Faces

✂ Activity

Directions: Cut out and show to students.

FEELINGS

Lesson 59: My Feelings Are Part of Me!

☞ Overview

During this lesson the class creates a class mural which shows the many feelings we all have, some that we like and some that we do not like. The children are guided to understand that all their feelings are a part of who they are.

☞ Grade Level

1st

☞ Materials

- Large block letters M and E made from bulletin board paper or poster board. (They need to be big enough for individual class pictures to be glued onto.)
- Drawing paper and markers for each student- To fit more easily on the ME letters the drawing paper should be 8.5 by 11 cut in half.
- *Today I Feel Silly* by Jamie Lee Curtis, available through Youthlight, Inc.

☞ Time Needed

30 minutes

☞ Objectives

- Students will learn the hand sign for feelings.
- Students will recognize the presence of comfortable and uncomfortable feelings in everyone.
- Students will illustrate feelings for a class mural.

☞ Procedures

- Teach student the hand sign for feelings.
- Ask students:
  - What are some of our feelings? Write their answers on the board including: Sad, Silly, Angry, Cranky, Excited, Happy, Scared
  - Do we like some feelings better than others? Why is that?
  - Can someone feel happy all the time? Why or why not?
  - When something sad happens is it all right to cry about it?
  - Who can we talk to when our feelings are bothering us?

- Give out drawing paper and ask children to pick one of the feelings on the board they want to illustrate. Ask for volunteers for certain feelings if necessary so that a variety of feelings are chosen.
- Have each child write "Sometimes I, _____,feel_____.

  Name   *Feeling Word*

  at the top of the page. Give students time to draw a picture of themselves having that particular feeling. As they are working you can walk around helping when necessary and talking with them about their pictures.
- Collect pictures and glue them all on the big block letters M-E that you have brought. Display in a prominent place in the hall or classroom.
- Review the hand sign for feelings in closing lesson. Remind children that we all have many different feelings every day and that is what makes us special.

☞ Discussion Questions

- How can you help yourself feel better when you are experiencing a feeling you do not like?
- How can you help a friend feel better?
- Is there a certain person in your life who always makes you feel better when you are sad? Who?

☞ Variations

- Give each student the option to share his or her drawing with the class, reading his or her sentence and explaining his or her feeling.
- Group students according to the feeling they chose and let them share their pictures and feelings with others in this small group setting.
- Make a graph of feelings to correlate a math lesson with the feelings lesson, showing how many students drew a particular feeling experience.

Lesson 60: The Colors of Feelings

☞ Overview

This lesson engages children's imaginations as they are asked to connect different colors to different feelings. The creation of a chain of feelings reinforces this concept and leaves a colorful reminder of the lesson in the classroom.

☞ Grade Level

2nd

☞ Materials

- *My Many Colored Days* by Dr. Seuss
- "Dr. Seuss' Many Colored Feelings" worksheet for each student
- Construction paper links in the following colors: bright red, bright blue, brown, yellow, gray, orange, green, purple, pink, black (You will need as many links as you have children in the class therefore some colors will be used more than once. Each child will have one link.)

☞ Time Needed

30 minutes

☞ Objectives

- Students will learn the hand sign for feelings.
- Students will associate different feelings with colors.
- Students will construct a colored chain of feelings.

☞ Procedures

- Teach the hand sign for feelings. Tell students that today we are going to have fun thinking about feelings as if they were colors. Put a list of some feeling words on the board to get them to start thinking along this line.
- Review some of their favorite Dr. Seuss book titles. Tell them that Dr. Seuss wrote the words to the book we are going to read today, but he died before he could illustrate it. Two other artists did the illustrations in this book, and that is why the pictures do not look like Dr. Seuss' other books.

- Ask students to pay attention to the different colors and feelings Dr. Seuss mentions as you read.
- After reading the book ask students to tell you some of the colors and feelings, and engage class in a discussion including the following points:
  - Do Dr. Seuss' feelings change? Do yours?
  - How do his different feelings cause his body to change as well?
  - What does he mean by a mixed up day?
  - Do you ever have a mixed up day?
  - Do we like some of our feelings more than others?
- Give out the different colored chain links and the "Dr. Seuss' Many Colored Feelings" worksheets. Review with children what each color means to Dr. Seuss. Ask them to think of an event or situation that makes them feel that color. Help them write that event or situation on their chain link.
- Staple all links together signifying that is how a class is, full of many individuals with many different feelings. Put the chain in a prominent place in the classroom.
- Remind children that feelings change during the month, week, day, hour, and minute. We do not need to assume that just because we feel low or sad one moment we will feel that way all day. There are lots of things we can do to help ourselves feel better.
- Elicit ideas of what we can do to help uncomfortable feelings change. Include: talk about them, exercise, draw, read, play a game, listen to music, write in a journal, take a nap, and play with a pet or favorite toy.
- Review the hand sign for feelings.

☞ Discussion Questions

- What is your favorite thing to do when you are feeling sad? Do you think this is everyone's favorite thing to do?
- Who are some trusted adults you can talk to when your feelings are mixed up?
- Dr. Seuss lived overlooking the ocean when he wrote this book. Have you ever noticed the different colors of the ocean water? How could this fact have helped Dr. Seuss in writing this book?

☞ Variations

- Using the words to Dr. Seuss' book, *My Many Colored Days*, ask the students to illustrate the pages themselves. Let this be a class project so that different pages are illustrated by different students. Include this diversity of illustrations in the discussion of the different feelings we all have.
- Have colored chain links available for students to add to the chain when they wish, allowing it to get longer with the many colors a concrete sign of our different, changing feelings.

Lesson 60: The Colors of Feelings

 **Activity**

Directions: Copy and give to each student.

DR. SEUSS' MANY COLORED FEELINGS

COLOR	FEELING
Bright Red	Peppy/Energetic
Bright Blue	Free As A Bird
Brown	Slow and Down
Yellow	Busy/Active
Gray	Quiet/Still
Orange	Playful
Green	Cool/Quiet
Purple	Sad
Pink	Happy
Black	Mad/Loud

Adapted from Seuss, Dr. My Many Colored Days. Knopf, 1996.

✎ Lesson 60: The Colors of Feelings

✂ Activity

Directions: Copy on colored construction paper or make your own.

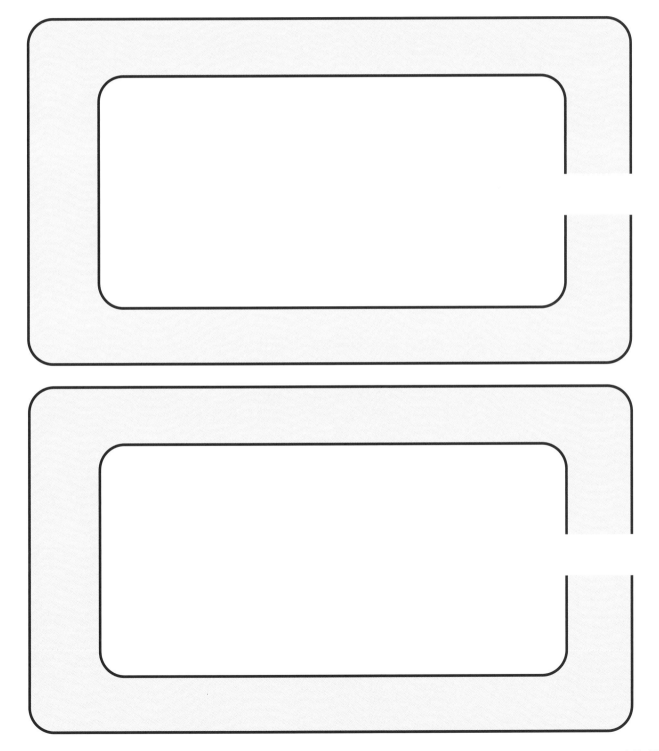

Lesson 61: Musical Feelings

☞ Overview

In this lesson the children play a classroom game which gives them a fun opportunity to express feelings. The lesson also creates more understanding between classmates as they hear other students' feelings expressed.

☞ Grade Level

3rd

☞ Materials

- 24 pieces of the same color construction paper with one of the following written on each piece of paper: Sad, Happy, Jealous, Embarrassed, Proud, Afraid, Excited, Shy, Lonely, Bored, Silly, Disappointed, Impatient, Discouraged, Angry, Thankful, Frustrated, Make a funny face, Jump up and down, Ask a friend a question, Whistle, Free Space, Free Space, Free Space
- CD player with CD of lively music
- *A Cup Full of Feeling* Worksheet

☞ Time Needed

30 minutes

☞ Objectives

- Students will learn the hand sign for feelings.
- Students will identify their own feelings and what causes them.
- Students will understand that all their classmates have similar feelings.

☞ Procedures

- Teach the hand sign for feelings. Tell students that today we are going to play a game while we learn about our feelings, a very important part of who we are.
- Put 24 pieces of paper face down on the floor without letting the students see what they say. Lay them in a circle or pattern around the desks as room allows.
- Ask for 5 volunteers to come to the front of the room, and instruct each student to stand beside one piece of paper. (If you can laminate these papers they will last longer and students can stand on them and not beside them.)

- Start the music, and instruct the students to walk around the circle or down the path of papers, stopping when you stop the music. One by one each student will turn over the piece of paper they are standing beside. If it is a feeling word they will read the word and share a time they felt that way. (Students can always pass if they do not want to share). If the paper tells them to do something they will follow the command, and if the paper is blank they will do nothing.
- Ask for another 5 volunteers until you have given every student a chance to play.
- Process the activity with the students by asking them:
  - Did one of your classmates surprise you with anything they said?
  - Do you feel like you have similar feelings to your classmates?
  - Are all our feelings ones we like to have?
  - How can we change our feelings from ones we don't like to ones we do?
  - Why are feelings so important?
  - How often do our feelings change in a week? A day? An hour? A minute?
- Review the hand sign for feelings, and encourage students to continue being aware of their feelings, and how important they are in their lives.

☞ Discussion Questions

- What is your favorite feeling? Is it possible to feel this way all the time? Would you want to? Why or why not?
- What is the difference between feeling angry and feeling frustrated? Is it hard to tell the difference between feelings sometimes?
- What is one way you help yourself feel better when you are having an unpleasant feeling?

☞ Variations

- While you have the CD player going, take advantage of the power of music to express feelings. Play a variety of songs, some with words and some without, and ask the students to identify the feeling they associate with that particular song.
- Group students in small groups, and ask them to prepare a list of ten good things to do to help yourself feel better when you are sad or angry. Let each group share their list with the class and prepare a master list to reproduce and give to each student.

✎ Lesson 61: Cup of Feeling

Directions: Fill the cup with words that describe how you feel when you are around your friends.

✎ Lesson 61: Cup of Feeling

Directions: Cut these feeling words apart to fill the cup on previous page.

Sad	Silly
Happy	Disappointed
Jealous	Impatient
Embarrassed	Discouraged
Proud	Angry
Afraid	Thankful
Excited	Frustrated
Shy	_____
Lonely	_____
Bored	_____

Lesson 62: Water or Ice Cube?

👉 Overview

This lesson engages students as they recognize, claim, and write about their feelings. They have the optional opportunity to share their feelings with others as well.

👉 Grade Level

4th

👉 Materials

- Copy of "My Letter To Me" on the following page for each student
- Scratch paper for each small group
- Plastic (or real) ice cube and glass of water

👉 Time Needed

30 minutes

👉 Objectives

- Students will learn the hand sign for feelings.
- Students will recognize some of the many feelings they have.
- Students will understand how feelings can change.

👉 Procedures

- Teach the hand sign for feelings. Ask students how many feelings they think people have. Accept all guesses, for there is no "right" answer.
- Put students in groups of 3-4 and give them 5 minutes to list as many feeling words as they can on the scratch paper you have provided
- Ask each group to share their feeling words with the class. After each group has read their list, take up the lists and tally the total number of feelings the class thought of. Lead a short discussion on this number asking them if this is more or less than they thought initially, and if they think this is all the feelings people have. Challenge them to continue to add to their feelings vocabulary as they continue to grow and mature.

- Give each student a copy of "My Letter To Me." Instruct them to put their name(s) in the blank. They are to write a letter to themselves saying how they feel today and why. If they want to share their letter, put a check in the blank provided.
- Give students about 10 minutes to write their letters. After all letters have been written, collect them, and share the ones that have been checked.
- Tell students you will put the letters in a very safe place and bring them with you next time you come to the class (or on a designated day in two-three weeks). You will return them to the writer, and you want them to read them again and think about how they feel then. Better? Worse? Same?
- Help them understand that feelings are not static like an ice cube, but fluid like water. Display the ice cube and glass of water as you continue sharing. Feelings flow, go places, and change shape from hour to hour, day to day. When you are having a feeling you don't like, remember this because this uncomfortable feeling will not last forever.

☞ Discussion Questions

- Can you think of a time when you felt like a certain feeling would last forever? Did it? Would you like to share this time with the class?
- What do you know now about your feelings that you did not know a year ago?
- Do you think this means that you will continue to learn about yourself and your feelings as you grow?
- How did you feel as you wrote your letter? Was it difficult to express your feelings on paper?

☞ Variations

- Continue the lesson having students share ideas as a small group and then as a class of ways to help themselves and others feel better when they need to.
- Give a homework assignment for students to think of additional metaphors for feelings. These metaphors will need to imply change, flexibility, and fluidity like water, the one used in the lesson.

✎ Lesson 62: My Letter To Me

OUR FEELINGS ARE MORE LIKE WATER THAN ICE, THEY FLOW AND CHANGE.

✎ Lesson 62: My Letter To Me

Directions: Fill in the blanks.

Dear _____,
Put your name here.

Right now I feel _____. **I feel this**
Write a feeling word here.

way because _____

_____

_____

_____.

When I am having a feeling I don't like, I can _____

_____

_____

_____.

Love,

_____
Your name here

☐ **Yes, I am willing to share my letter.**

Lesson 63: Thinking and Feeling

 ## Overview

This lesson introduces the concept of the connection between feelings and thoughts to the students. They are helped to see that how they think about what happens to them can influence their feelings about the situation.

 ## Grade Level

5th

 ## Materials

- "Thinking and Feeling" worksheet on the following page for each student

 ## Time Needed

30 minutes

 ## Objectives

- Students will learn the hand sign for feelings.
- Students will learn the relationship between thoughts and feelings.
- Students will explore events in their lives that could be thought about in new ways.

Procedures

- Teach the hand sign for feelings. See how many feeling words the students can call out for you to list on the board in 2 minutes.
- Ask students, "Can you choose your feelings like you choose your flavor of ice cream?" Allow for short discussion. Tell them that today we are going to prove that at times we can choose our feelings, and you are going to prove it to them.
- Distribute the Thinking and Feeling worksheets. Process with them the first example, role playing a student bumping into you in the hall. Demonstrate how this same event can produce very different feelings depending on what you think about what happened.
- Give students time to go through the other examples individually, writing down their thoughts and feelings for each one.

- Have class discussion on what they discovered, giving them time to share the events they thought of for number 5 on worksheet.
- Review the hand sign for feelings.

☞ Discussion Questions

- What feelings are the hardest for you to stop and think about?
- What can you do to help yourself think and keep your feelings under control?
- How does it help us to think more positively about a situation so that our feelings can change?

☞ Variations

- Have students role play the four events on the worksheets, while you verbalize the different thoughts they could have.
- Put up a visual reminder of today's lesson in the room, such as a sign which reads "Think about how you are feeling." Refer the students to this sign when you see one of them getting upset. Give them a quiet, private place in the room to go to think and calm down if necessary.

✎ Lesson 63: Thinking and Feeling

Directions: Did you know you can change your feelings about a particular event by changing your thoughts about what happened? Below are some examples of this. One possible thought and corresponding feeling you might have is given. You are to think about the event in another way, and write down the feeling that would go with those thoughts. Notice how the event stays the same, but when thoughts about it change, so do your feelings. We will do the first one together. For number 5 think of another example of an event, and fill in two possible ways to think about it and the corresponding feelings that would go with those thoughts.

EVENT	THOUGHT	FEELING
1. Someone bumps into you in the hall.	He or she did it on purpose.	Anger, Revenge
Someone bumps into you in the hall.	He or she is clumsy and in a hurry.	Mild annoyance and forgiveness
2. A good friend does not come to your birthday party.	He or she is mad at you or doesn't like you.	Confusion, Anger, Hurt
A good friend does not come to your birthday party.		
3. Your team loses a game.	Everyone thinks you are on the worst team in the league.	Discouragement, Shame
Your team loses a game.		
4. Your teacher doesn't call on you.	The teacher likes other students more than you.	Resentment, Jealousy
Your teacher doesn't call on you.		

COUNSELOR'S CORNER

Dear Parents,

Today your child learned the hand sign for feelings in our guidance lesson. Accepting and understanding our range of feelings is a crucial part of healthy emotional development for all of us. There are many ways we can help our children in this process. One way we can help is to make them aware that all of us have a variety of feelings - some we like and some we do not. Children also need to know that feelings change, and that there are strategies we can use to help ourselves feel better.

As a parent, you can help your children with this emotional development by encouraging them to talk about their feelings, and by listening as they talk. They should never be made to feel guilty for having a particular feeling, but should be encouraged to share them with people who love them. This nonjudgmental sharing helps all children learn to handle the uncomfortable feelings, and to know that talking about them can make them feel better.

Ask your child to show you the hand sign for feelings and try using it with them from time to time as you observe both comfortable and uncomfortable feelings arising in them. They will be glad to know you understand the complex but normal display of the many feelings they have every day.

Sincerely,

Your School Counselor

© YouthLight Inc.

RESOURCES

Beaumont, Karen. *I Like Myself*. Scholastic 2004.

Berenstain, Stan and Jan. *Trouble At School*. Random House. 1986.

Berenstain, Stan and Jan. *Trouble With Friends*. Random House. 1986.

Bourgeois, Paulette and Clark, Brenda. *Franklin Fibs*. Scholastic. 1991.

Bowman, Bob. *102 Mind Bogglers*. YouthLight, Inc. 2005.

Burnett, Karen. *Simon's Hook*. GR Publishing. 1999.

Cain, Janan. *The Way I Feel*. Parenting Press. 2000..

Costello. Elaine. *Concise American Sign Language Dictionary*. Bantam Books, 2000.

Curtis, Jamie Lee. *When I Was Little*. Scholastic. 1993.

Curtis, Jamie Lee. *Today I Feel Silly*. Joanna Cotler Books, 1998.

Gardner, Howard. Frames of Mind. *The Theory of Multiple Intelligences*. Basic Books. 1993.

Gatewood, Betts and Senn, Diane. Bee Your Best. YouthLight, Inc. 2001.

Gatewood, Betts. Counseling By Power Point. YouthLight, Inc. 2005.

Holland, John L. *Making Vocational Choices: A Theory of Vocational Personalities and Work Environments*. Psychological Assessment Resources Inc. 1997.

Judd, Naomi. *Love Can Build A Bridge*. Harper Collins. 1999.

Kaiser, Cecily. *If You're Angry and You Know It*. Scholastic. 2004.

Krensky, Stephen. *How Santa Got His Job*. Alladin. 2002.

Lovell, Patty. Stand Tall, *Molly Lou Melon*. Scholastic. 2001.

Parramore, Hopke, and Drier. *Children's Dictionary of Occupations*. Meridian. 2004.

Pilkey, Dav. *The Paperboy*. Scholastic. 1996.

Seuss, Dr. *My Many Colored Days*. Alfred Knopf. 1996.